— THE HOUSE PARTY —

National
Trust

THE
HOUSE
PARTY

A Short History of Leisure,
Pleasure and the
Country House Weekend

ADRIAN TINNISWOOD

ff

FABER & FABER

First published in 2019
by Faber & Faber Limited
Bloomsbury House
74–77 Great Russell Street
London WC1B 3DA

Typeset by Donald Sommerville
Printed and bound in the UK by CPI Group Ltd, Croydon CR0 4YY

A CIP record for this book
is available from the British Library

ISBN 978–0–571–35096–4

2 4 6 8 10 9 7 5 3 1

For the Sea Rod Inn, with thanks

Contents

INTRODUCTION

IN STATELY
CONCLAVE MET

The country house party occupies a special place in British culture. Whether it involves jazz and cocaine, or sherry and stilted conversation, or even a body in the library and the arrival of Miss Marple, the weekend spent in a moated manor house or a palatial Palladian villa has come to epitomise the privileged lifestyle of a tiny minority in an age which has passed. And while we might celebrate its passing, a little part of us still wishes we could have been there at the wake.

The golden age of the house party began during Queen Victoria's reign, when her son and his cronies were enthusiastically drinking, gambling and fornicating their way through country houses all over Britain. It ended half a century later, when drinking, gambling and fornicating had to take second place to fighting fascism. And it comes as no surprise that the period coincided with a relaxation of social convention which allowed the new rich and figures from the arts to mix more freely in traditional landed society than ever before, challenging the old formalities. Nor should we ignore the fact that this golden age peaked in the years between the world wars, when the fusion of two lost generations – the one which had washed away its innocence in the blood of Flanders field and could never forget the sights it had seen, and the other whose guilt at being too young to fight left it eager to forget the sights it hadn't seen – turned the country house weekend into a game played by Bright Young Things and those who were less bright, perhaps, less young, but ultimately more enduring.

1

EARLY ARRIVALS

The country house has always attracted visitors. Queen Elizabeth I dropped in at Sir Thomas Lucy's Charlecote in the summer of 1572 during a tour of Warwickshire, and the following year she spent five days at Knole during a progress through Kent (although since Knole was then a royal house, she was technically both host and guest). In 1576 she spent a couple of days with Sir Thomas Gresham at Osterley in Middlesex, where she famously remarked that his new courtyard 'would appear more handsome if divided by a wall in the middle'.[1] Gresham summoned workmen from London and overnight they made the Queen's wish come true, leading the court wits to comment on some family problems that Gresham was having, saying it was easier to divide a house than it was to unite it.

More than a century later William of Orange visited Sir John Brownlow at Belton, his new house near Grantham in Lincolnshire. Brownlow showed the king such a good time, and left him with such a horrible hangover, that William couldn't face the feast that was provided for him when he arrived at Lincoln the next day. George III and

Queen Charlotte made a brief visit to the 1st Earl of Mount Edgcumbe at Cotehele in Cornwall in August 1789, whilst staying at Saltram over the border in Devon. 'A large hall full of old armour and swords', Charlotte wrote in her diary.[2]

Unwary guests who spent a night at Seaton Delaval in the eighteenth century found themselves falling victim to some rather trying practical jokes. Their hosts, the Delavals, fitted out their magnificent Northumberland mansion with a range of elaborate devices, all designed to embarrass, confuse and humiliate. For example, having retired for the night, a visitor might be in the middle of undressing when mechanical hoists raised their bedroom walls like theatrical scenery, exposing them to view and, presumably, to ridicule. Or they could be wakened abruptly from dreamless sleep as their bed was lowered into a bath of cold water by a system of ropes and pulleys operated by a Delaval lurking next door. A guest who had drunk too much might be put to bed in the dark; when they eventually roused themselves the next morning, they would be astonished to discover they were lying on the ceiling of their bedroom: the room's furnishings were inverted, with chairs and tables stuck to the ceiling and a chandelier standing up in the middle of the floor.[3]

Friends, neighbours, relations, even passing celebrities might arrive at one's country house, sometimes with little or no notice. Mary Elizabeth Lucy and her husband George were still in bed at Charlecote one morning in January 1828 when they heard the ringing of their front door bell, and a maid came to tell them that Sir Walter Scott and his daughter were downstairs. 'Don't I remember our hurry to get dressed', Mary Elizabeth recalled, 'when we heard *who* it was that had arrived and were waiting for permission to see the house.'[4]

Scott only stayed for a couple of hours, in spite of being pressed to stay longer. But in a slightly later age, when the rail network was in its infancy and roads were often impassable in bad weather, an extended visit was the norm. Typical of the early house party was the occasion in the 1850s when Mary Elizabeth Lucy, now widowed, and her daughter Carry had 'a charming expedition' to Eywood in Herefordshire, where they were the guests of Lord and Lady Langdale for a fortnight. There was a large party, including a Count Teleki, a Hungarian fortune-hunter who was courting Lady Langdale's daughter and who subsequently married her, only to leave her three days after the wedding, announcing as he went that he already had a wife and family in Hungary. In fact it was quite a cosmopolitan group, with an unnamed Polish nobleman, a virtuoso gypsy violinist named Edvard Remery, and Mary Elizabeth's Welsh harp teacher Mr Thomas among the guests. The Langdales were good hosts: there were carriages and horses to drive or ride, picnics, a flower show, dancing, 'and two harps upon which Mr Thomas and I played duets'.[5]

One tends to assume that mid-Victorian house parties were sedate affairs. Not this one. In the course of a long walk through a meadow, the group came to a ditch, which they all managed to negotiate except for a Miss Bickersteth, who declared she couldn't possibly jump it. Count Teleki promptly lay down at full length across the ditch and invited her to use him as a bridge, which she did, 'and we all screamed with laughing'. After dinner Monsieur Remery stood at the top of the stairs and played his 'wild wizard-like music', while the rest of the men showed off by leaping over chairs. Teleki and the Polish baron challenged the others to balance on the top banister rail of the main staircase, and Mr Thomas, his manhood impugned by these foreign upstarts, immediately declared he could do it. He couldn't. In fact he fell on Mary Elizabeth's head, 'and knocked me down flat on my knees, most fortunately for him as had he fallen on the marble floor in all probability he would have been killed'. Everyone (except Mary Elizabeth and Mr Thomas, presumably) laughed so loud and so long 'that the hall rang again with their peals of excitement'.[6]

In December 1901 Buckingham Palace announced that Edward VII and Queen Alexandra would be making a royal visit to the island of Ireland, then all still part of the United Kingdom. Building on Queen Victoria's successful visit of April 1900, the plan was for the royal couple to spend a week in Dublin, staying at the Viceregal Lodge in Phoenix Park, the summer residence of the Lord Lieutenant of Ireland. (He had to move out.) Although this was to be a very public occasion, the King and Queen also planned to make two semi-private visits, one to the Duke and Duchess of Devonshire at Lismore Castle down in County Waterford, and the other to the Marquess and Marchioness of Londonderry at Mount Stewart on the Ards Peninsula in County Down, fifteen miles from Belfast.

In the event the King's ill health – a gastric abscess in June 1902 led to the postponement of his coronation – meant that the visit didn't take place until July 1903. But when it came, it was a nerve-racking experience for the Londonderrys, who played host to the King and Queen over the weekend of 25 and 26 July. Edward could be a demanding guest, never slow to make his displeasure known; as one of his courtiers remarked, he was always ready to forget his rank, 'as long as everyone else remembers it'.[7] On informal occasions, he expected to choose the guests invited to a house party, and he expected them to include his current mistress. And he brought quite an entourage: when he stayed at Rufford Abbey in Nottinghamshire, for example, he brought with him a valet, a footman, a brusher, two equerries with valets, two telephonists, two chauffeurs, and an Arab boy to make coffee.

The visit to Mount Stewart was emphatically *not* an informal party. The King and Queen travelled up from Dublin in a special train fitted with a drawing room, dining room, smoking room, a boudoir for the Queen, 'and full culinary equipment'.[8] Crowds cheered them through every station on the route, and they were preceded by an army of journalists in a specially chartered train, although the plan to report on the royal couple's arrival at Mount Stewart was thwarted when the press train was accidentally sent to Belfast instead. The Londonderrys gave up their own rooms for the King and Queen, having had them redecorated and upholstered for the occasion, with white and gold damask specially woven in Belfast for Alexandra's rooms, and linen woven and embroidered by the women and girls on the estate for the King's. Big though Mount Stewart is, there wasn't room for everyone, and some of the royal household servants were accommodated in tents in the grounds.

The packed royal schedule, most of which took place in awful weather, began on the Saturday afternoon, when the King and Lord Londonderry were driven ten miles down to Portaferry by motor car to board a steam launch, which set off across Strangford Lough so that the King could spend half an hour at Lord de Ros's country house, Oldcourt. Back in Portaferry the royal car wouldn't start, and the King was left to stand in torrential rain and failing light, quietly smoking a cigar, as a posse of police and locals pushed it to the top of the steep hill, at which point the chauffeur finally managed to get it going. It broke down again on the way home but the King, who was an enthusiastic motorist, seems to have taken everything in good part.

That evening the Londonderrys hosted a dinner party for the great and the good of Ulster, and the next morning, after a service in the Mount Stewart private chapel with a sermon from the Primate of Ireland, the King and Queen summoned the Marchioness to their sitting room and presented her with 'a most lovely bracelet, their two miniatures set in diamonds, with the Royal crown and cyphers, and green enamel shamrocks on the sides'.[9] The rest of the day was spent in careering through the countryside of County Down. According to reporters – who by now had caught up with the royal party – there was quite a convoy:

A pilot car went first, and in it were Lord Londonderry and the Duke of Abercorn [a prominent Irish landowner and one of Ireland's leading Unionists]. The next car, of a large brougham shape and covered with a canvas hood, was driven by the Earl of Shrewsbury, the hereditary Lord High Steward of Ireland. On his left sat the King, who was wearing a brown overcoat and a brown bowler hat. Immediately behind sat the Queen and Lady Londonderry.[10]

Three more cars followed, containing Princess Victoria and members of the royal household. They paid a visit to the dowager Marchioness of Dufferin at nearby Clandeboye House, and then meandered home along the coast. On Monday, after each planting an oak tree in the garden, Edward and Alexandra were back on the royal train for a state entrance into Belfast. The King was resplendent in an admiral's uniform with the ribbon of the Order of St Patrick sashed over his shoulder. 'The Queen followed, smiling as ever, in an exquisite gown of Irish poplin lace, heliotrope in tint.'[11]

In complete contrast to the regal pomp of the King's visit to Mount Stewart was the weekend he spent in June 1909 at Polesden Lacey in Surrey where, as the press put it, 'A small party of his intimate friends were invited to meet him.'[12] His hostess on this occasion was the indefatigable Margaret Greville, the illegitimate and immensely wealthy daughter of the Scottish brewer William McEwan. Margaret had bought Polesden Lacey, a substantial Regency villa recently modernised by its previous owner, in 1906 with an £80,000 gift from her father; and over the next two years she and her husband Ronald, a Conservative politician, brought in the architects of the Ritz Hotel, Charles Mewès and Arthur J. Davis, to create a series of opulent interiors. Mrs Greville wanted modern convenience – there were eighteen bedrooms and eleven en suite bathrooms – and she wanted luxury. 'I want a room I can entertain maharajahs in,' she told her architects.[13]

And, she might have added, a room fit for a king. The Grevilles were friendly with Edward VII, having entertained him several times at Reigate Priory, a country house in Surrey which they had rented occasionally. Margaret was sensitive to the King's requirements, making sure that his mistress Alice Keppel was invited on such occasions and that her room was not too far distant from his. 'I don't follow people to their bedrooms,' Margaret once remarked: 'It's what they do outside them that is important' – a sentiment not shared by either Edward VII or Alice Keppel.[14] As a single-minded social hostess, one of the reasons for Mrs Greville's expensive refurbishment of Polesden Lacey was her determination to build on this royal friendship. She and her husband created a private suite for the King at Polesden, furnished in pale blue-green silk with a carved and gilded double bed.

Edward VII's inaugural visit to Polesden Lacey was planned for the summer of 1908, but Ronald Greville died quite suddenly that April, aged only forty-three, and the visit had to be postponed. It eventually took place in June 1909 when, as newspaper reports put it, 'His Majesty the King honoured the Hon. Mrs Ronald Greville by spending the last week-end at Polesden Lacey, near Dorking.'[15] Edward motored down from Buckingham Palace late on the afternoon of Saturday 5 June, to be greeted by a small party of guests.

There were eighteen in the house party altogether. They included Mrs Greville's father William McEwan; Mrs Keppel, her husband George and their daughter Sonia; the Countess of Dudley, with whom Edward had

had a brief fling in the 1890s; and Randolph Churchill's sister Lady Sarah Wilson, who tended to go wherever Alice Keppel went.

Margaret brought a photographer over from Reigate to take a group photograph of the party looking relaxed on the terrace in front of her house: the King sat in his homburg and overcoat, smiling with a cigar in his hand and his dog Caesar at his feet.* Mrs Greville sat next to him, looking pleased with herself. After the King left on Monday morning, she circulated the photograph to the newspapers.

Three weeks later the papers announced that the Grand Duke Michael of Russia and his wife Sophie of Merenberg, were spending the weekend at Polesden Lacey, 'where they are the guests of Hon. Mrs Ronald Greville'.[16] House parties were routinely used by great tacticians like Mrs Greville to maintain and improve social standing, and the press was happy to play its part. 'What a wonderful hostess Mrs Ronald Greville is,' gushed the *Tatler*'s gossip columnist in one of the many 'news' stories that appeared

---

* Like his master, the dog frequently went in pursuit of whatever took his fancy. He wore a brown leather collar with a brass name-plate engraved with just five words: 'I belong to the King'.

about her entertaining. 'She always manages to get that perfect mixture of the great and the beautiful, and the distinguished and the clever, and the noble, with no uncongenial element, at her house parties at Polesden Lacey.'[17]

2

WHO TO ASK

'There are certain rules to be observed in the writing of invitations that cannot be transgressed,' declared the author of a classic etiquette manual for the socially insecure, *Manners and Customs of Polite Society*, before going on to devote an entire chapter of her book to the correct way to give invitations, and another to the correct way of responding to them. 'To widely depart from any of these received canons of etiquette is to commit a decided solecism and to discover an utter unfitness for the desired social rank.' Failing to reply in the third person, for example, 'would imply ignorance of the rudiments of social and grammatical rules'.[1]

By the inter-war years, when an established rail network and a dramatic increase in car ownership meant that the weekend country house party as a social phenomenon was at its zenith, there were plenty of households where extreme formality still prevailed. But the Great War had changed people. The younger ones, both those who had fought and those who had not, were less patient in their pursuit of pleasure, and the advent of the telephone and the importing of more relaxed manners from America meant that Edwardian conventions were looking increasingly outmoded. Laura, Lady Troubridge, a baronet's wife whose books on etiquette and entertaining ('to help you on your social way') were bestsellers in the 1920s and 1930s, announced in 1939 that 'The new etiquette is informal . . . you will not be doing the wrong thing if you accept this new spirit, and waive any petty, cramping little rules which were intended for another, and far more formal, age.'[2]

By the time that Lady Troubridge was announcing the new etiquette, invitations to join a house party usually stipulated that guests should arrive late on Saturday afternoon and leave after breakfast on Monday. 'They were never called weekends,' recalled the Duchess of Buccleuch. 'They were called Saturday-to-Mondays . . . It was supposed to be awfully non-U to call them weekends.'[3] But the rules did vary from house to house: Friday-to-Sundays were becoming increasingly popular in the 1930s, especially in social circles where the men – and even the women – had jobs which meant they had to be in an office in the City on Monday morning. Shooting parties tended to happen mid-week, and for those with Scottish estates, a visit might last for several weeks. At Ickworth in Suffolk dinner parties were something of a rarity, for the oddest of reasons. 'There were lodge-keepers at each of the three

– 18 –

entrances,' recalled Phyllis, daughter of the 4th Marquess of Bristol: 'It was not easy to ask people to dinner, because the lodge-keeper would usually have gone to bed by the time they left, so they could not get out.'[4]

Crucially, an invitation should stipulate not only the day on which to arrive, but also the time of arrival. Woe betide the guest who didn't stick to the schedule. 'Nothing is more annoying for the host who occupies a remote house', declared the author of yet another mid-century etiquette manual, 'than to have to make several long and fruitless journeys [to the railway station] to pick up a guest.'[5] Actually, one thing was more annoying: the guests who outstayed their welcome. Prudent hosts and hostesses usually made it clear in their invitation how long a visit was expected to last.

Some families didn't like entertaining at all. Harold Nicolson and his wife Vita Sackville-West often had guests to stay at Long Barn in the Kent village of Sevenoaks Weald, 'our own nestling home amidst the meadows'. When they moved to Sissinghurst in 1932, however, they decided it was to be a private sanctuary for them, their two boys and, when the other was away from home, for the discreet reception of one or other of their many lovers. There were no guest rooms, and Nigel Nicolson later recalled that his mother insisted on him and his brother

Ben sharing a bedroom until they were students 'because, she explained, if we had a bedroom each and one of us was away, Lady Colefax might find out and invite herself for the weekend'.[6]

Vita had no such scruples when it came to accepting invitations. She often stayed with Leonard and Virginia Woolf at Monk's House, their sixteenth-century cottage in the Sussex village of Rodmell. In 1926 the Woolfs installed a bathroom and lavatory with the some of the proceeds from Virginia's novel *Mrs Dalloway*. It was quite a novelty – Vita told Harold that Virginia and Leonard 'run upstairs every now and then and pull the plug just for the sheer fun of it.'[7] Visits to Vita's ancestral home, Knole, became less frequent after her father's death in 1928. Excluded from inheriting Knole because of her sex, she felt its loss keenly, and even more so after her uncle, the 4th Lord Sackville, gave it to the National Trust in 1947 during the great wave of estate transfers that took place in the 1940s, when the uncertainties of war, followed by the arrival of Clement Attlee's Labour government, led dozens of owners to negotiate with the Trust in the hope of being rescued from financial disaster and socialism. 'Knole should have been mine, mine, mine,' Vita told Harold. 'We were meant for each other.'[8]

Knole was one of those great country houses where

Edwardian standards of formal behaviour prevailed well into the 1930s. Wallis Simpson, who spent several weekends there with her husband Ernest, found the Sackvilles hopelessly stuffy. The relaxed atmosphere of the Prince of Wales's Fort Belvedere in Windsor Great Park, where the Simpsons were first invited for a Saturday-to-Monday in 1931, was much more to her taste – in so many ways. ('What could you possibly want that queer old place for?' George V asked his son. 'Those damn week-ends, I suppose.'[9])

Different country houses attracted different kinds of guest. There were political houses, literary houses, hunting houses, downright weird houses. Some drew their weekend guests almost exclusively from the county, or from extended family networks; others could be depended on to provide celebrities for every occasion, from film stars to establishment painters to government ministers. In the 1930s the Londonderrys, who usually spent August and September at Mount Stewart, entertained notable figures ranging from the Duke of Gloucester, who flew back to England in his private aeroplane, to Prime Minster Ramsay MacDonald and, notoriously, German ambassador Joachim von Ribbentrop, dubbed 'the Londonderry Herr', who fell overboard when they took him sailing on Strangford Lough.

Royals were always popular – or almost always. Loelia, Duchess of Westminster remembered that when Prince Arthur of Connaught stayed at Eaton Hall, 'He was a bit of a bore – and Princess Arthur, an even bigger bore. The only subject she seemed able to talk about was nursing the sick.'[10] 'No hostess of our time stands higher in the esteem of royalty than the Hon. Mrs Ronald Greville,' gushed the press, after she had been invited to attend the first private dinner party to be given after the accession of George VI and Queen Elizabeth at Buckingham Palace in 1937.[11] She was 'popular with all the members of the Royal Family', according to the gossip columns.[12]

The engagement of Lord Louis Mountbatten, great-grandson of Queen Victoria, and Edwina Ashley was settled during a house party at Polesden Lacey in 1921, and when George V's second son, the Duke of York, was seen with Elizabeth Bowes-Lyon at weekends at Polesden and at dinner parties at Mrs Greville's London house, the press began to ask if the next royal engagement would be another Greville coup. In fact Elizabeth finally accepted the duke's proposal during a house party at her father's Hertfordshire country house, St Paul's Walden Bury; but the couple had fond memories of Polesden and they accepted Mrs Greville's offer to put it at their disposal for their honeymoon in 1923. Their hostess discreetly retreated to her Mayfair mansion for the duration, but she traded on the status brought by that honeymoon for the rest of her life.

Sometimes the royal visit was a brief one. In July 1946 the 10th Earl of Stamford entertained George VI and Queen Elizabeth to lunch at his country seat, Dunham Massey in Cheshire. They left afterwards for Chester, but not before the earl, a reclusive bachelor with antiquarian interests, had, according to the *Tatler*, given his royal guests 'an outline of the history of the ancient residence, and showed them some of the historical relics collected in the Hall'.[13] He had good reason to be proud of them, having spent years in buying back paintings and silver which had gone out of the family at the turn of the century.

If one couldn't attract the British royal family to one's house – and even if one could – there were other options. The Earl of Stamford played host to Emperor Haile Selassie at Dunham in 1938, during the latter's exile from Ethiopia. Lord and Lady Sackville managed to lure the King and Queen of Siam to Knole in 1934. Fourteen years earlier Mrs Greville netted Alfonso XIII of Spain and his queen, Victoria Eugenie – 'the Spains', as the *Tatler* called them with a cheerful disregard for protocol.[14] Edith, Lady Londonderry entertained the Spains' daughters, the *infantas* Beatrice and Maria Christina (great-granddaughters of Queen Victoria), at Mount Stewart on several occasions. In the summer of 1931 the *infantas* were treated to a fête arranged by Edith, with pageants, a dress parade and a children's riding competition which the Spanish princesses were asked to judge. 'The distinguished visitors were dressed alike in white silk tennis frocks, grass-green tweed coats and white berets,' reported the press; 'Many of the leading citizens of Belfast and counties Antrim and Down were present.'[15] In 1935 Christmas guests of the Howard de Waldens at Chirk Castle near Wrexham included Prince Alonso and Prince Ataúlfo of Bourbon-Saxe-Coburg-Gotha, also great-grandchildren of Queen Victoria but in a different line (their mother was Beatrice of Saxe-Coburg-Gotha and their father Alfonso of Bourbon-Orléans, a cousin of Alfonso XIII).

Nancy Astor, the queen of society hostesses in the 1920s and 1930s, welcomed a galaxy of stars – politicians, celebrities, writers, actors – to Cliveden, the Buckinghamshire country house given to her and her husband Waldorf as a wedding present by Waldorf's father, the 1st Viscount Astor. In Cliveden's heyday it was common for as many as forty guests to arrive for the weekend. They might include George Bernard Shaw, Henry Ford, Charlie Chaplin, Gandhi, Charles Lindbergh, Lawrence of Arabia and half the British Cabinet.

By the later 1930s Cliveden had acquired a reputation as a political house, perhaps even *the* political house. Many of the Astors' regular guests were journalists: Geoffrey Dawson, editor of *The Times*; James Garvin, editor of the *Observer* (which Astor owned); Robert Barrington-Ward, chief leader-writer on *The Times*. But active politicians also came along to enjoy the Astors' lavish hospitality. Harold Nicolson spent a weekend at Cliveden in June 1936 and found himself in the company of the Foreign Secretary, the Speaker of the House of Commons, an Oxford professor of political theory, a Liberal MP, a Conservative peer, the Canadian High Commissioner, Winston Churchill's aunt and a gaggle of forlorn Americans, Astor relations and assorted hangers-on.

Sections of the press saw the Astors and their friends as leading players in the horror that was unfolding across Europe in the late 1930s. It was the so-called Cliveden Set, the left-wing papers claimed, which had forced the resignation of Foreign Secretary Anthony Eden, who was opposed to Mussolini's expansionist policies. The Set was believed to have engineered his replacement by the pro-Hitler Lord Halifax, and to be pushing Prime Minister Chamberlain into appeasing the Nazis. When Chamberlain spent a weekend at Cliveden, the Labour politician Sir Stafford Cripps declared that 'The Cliveden set . . . are the people who are running policy today behind Neville Chamberlain and they are the people who would like to see Great Britain a Fascist State as well.'[16]

Was Cliveden a hotbed of appeasers and pro-Nazis? Not really. Nancy and Waldorf welcomed all sorts to their weekends. George Bernard Shaw, then pro-Stalin and a self-styled Communist, dismissed the furore about the Set as 'senseless', pointing out that 'I could prove that Cliveden is a nest of Bolshevism, or indeed of any other bee in the world's bonnet.'[17] But Dawson, Garvin, Nancy Astor and others of their friends *were* pro-German and remained so long after it was obvious that Hitler was a very bad man indeed. Nancy was an outspoken and bigoted anti-Semite. At different times and in different degrees, members of the Set believed that what Hitler did in pursuit of *Lebensraum* in eastern Europe was no business of Britain's and that the Nazis would prove a formidable bulwark against the creeping Bolshevism of the Soviet Union.

Harold Nicolson put his finger on the hubristic heart of the Cliveden Set in the spring of 1939. As war loomed, he railed at Nancy Astor for being one of those 'silly selfish hostesses' who do immense damage by giving the impression 'that foreign policy is decided in their own drawing-rooms'.[18]

3

MAKING AN ENTRANCE

On a cold January day in 1935 Henry 'Chips' Channon and his wife Honor drove for the weekend to Lord Brownlow's country home, Belton House near Grantham. They had just spent Christmas and New Year at Elveden, the enormous Suffolk mansion which belonged to Honor's father, the 2nd Earl of Iveagh, where Chicago-born Chips had revelled in the 'luxurious Edwardian atmosphere', and in the fact that he had been given a bedroom used by both Edward VII and George V; although he was embarrassed by the fact that in the middle of the night he had inadvertently smashed the chamber pot which had also, presumably, been used by both Edward VII and George V.[1] Apparently he made rather a habit of this: at the Roseberys' Mentmore Towers a few years earlier he managed to break a pot that once belonged to Napoleon. It carried the emperor's monogram.

The Channons' fellow house-guests at Belton were an illustrious bunch: Lord and Lady Weymouth (the future Marquis and Marchioness of Bath); Duff Cooper, Financial Secretary to the Treasury and an ardent anti-appeaser, and his wife, the beautiful actress and socialite

Lady Diana Cooper; and Piers Legh, equerry to the Prince of Wales, and his American wife Sarah.

Channon hadn't visited Belton before: he was impressed, describing it as 'built by Christopher Wren' (which it wasn't) and 'almost overfull of treasures' (which it was).[2] He was also impressed by his hosts, Perry and Katherine Brownlow, although he was less enthusiastic about some of the other guests: Piers Legh and his wife were 'frankly bores', he noted in his diary, although inveterate snob that he was, he also noted Legh's status as royal equerry.

The reason for the Belton house party was that the guests had been invited to a grand ball at Belvoir Castle, just the other side of Grantham. It was being given that night by the Duke and Duchess of Rutland for their teenage daughters, Ursula and Isabel.*

After dining at Belton the Brownlows and their guests drove over to Belvoir for the ball, which was a great success. Honor Channon wore her tiara; the 79-year-old dowager Duchess of Rutland looked suitably matriarchal, dressed

---

* Lady Diana Cooper was the aunt of Ursula and Isabel and, on paper at least, the daughter of the 8th Duke of Rutland. Her real father was Henry Cust, a cousin of her host at Belton, Perry Brownlow, 6th Lord Brownlow. It was a small world.

all in white and surrounded by her descendants, about thirty of them; and Chips was smitten with the Rutland girls, 'both dazzlers', and especially by the seventeen-year-old Isabel, 'a dream of romantic loveliness'.[3] But one of the more intriguing features of the day was the fact that the Channons were there at all. Country house weekends like this would scarcely have been possible a century earlier, when, for example, it took the Lucys two whole days to make the 140-mile journey from Charlecote to Mary Elizabeth Lucy's family home at Bodlewyddan, on the north coast of Wales. In 1935 the Channons could motor over from Elveden to Belton, a distance of ninety miles, and arrive in time for dinner before setting out on a thirty-mile round trip to Belvoir and back.

A prerequisite for a weekend house party in the country was the means to get to one's destination and back quickly and with a minimum of effort. Initially it was the rapid expansion of the rail network which provided this. By 1870, only forty years after the opening of the Liverpool and Manchester, the first modern railway, there were about 13,500 miles of track; in 1914 there were 20,000 miles. From 1868 until the mass closure of branch lines in the 1960s, the Verneys of Claydon in Buckinghamshire had their very own station, Verney Junction, which stood a few hundred yards from Claydon House. Nor was this uncommon (although the fact that it was named after the family was, but Sir Harry Verney was a big investor in the Aylesbury and Buckingham Railway, which built Verney Junction as its northern terminus). The Rothschilds of Waddesdon Manor had their own station from 1897, for example; and in Derbyshire, the Vernons of Sudbury had a station serving the village and the Hall.

By the early years of the twentieth century one could settle into a first-class carriage at Liverpool Street at 3.20 p.m. on Friday afternoon and arrive at Aylsham in Norfolk to be picked up and driven to Lord Lothian's Blickling Hall in time to change for dinner. House-guests at the Earl of Coventry's Croome Court could sit in their Mayfair flat on a Saturday morning and leaf through Bradshaw's *General Railway and Steam Navigation Guide*, confident that the 1.45 p.m. Great Western from Paddington would deposit them at Worcester Shrub Hill at 4.37; a telegram to Croome would ensure that the earl's chauffeur, Roland Newman, was waiting at the station to pick them up in a gleaming red Standard Twenty.

The conveyance which took a guest from railway station to country house varied according to the whims, resources and status of one's host. Domestic servants arriving at Worcester en route to Croome found themselves travelling not in the earl's Standard Twenty but in a smelly blue van, which was also used to take the Countess of Coventry's hounds to and from meets, and to collect offal and cheap cuts of meat to feed them. In contrast Sir Philip Sassoon, who entertained relentlessly at his two country houses, Port Lympne in Kent and Trent Park just north of London, sent his Rolls-Royce, which had a distinctive silver snake mascot perched on the bonnet. Well into the 1920s house-guests of the 5th Earl of Lonsdale would arrive at Penrith station in Westmorland to be greeted by a groom clad in buckskin breeches, high boots, a cloth coat in the Lonsdale yellow and a beaver hat. He conducted them to a coachman who waited in an open yellow landau drawn by a pair of cream-coloured horses, which conveyed them the six miles from Penrith to the earl's Lowther Castle. Their luggage followed on behind in a yellow van.

By the 1930s car ownership was running at one for every five households, and travelling down to the country by motor for the weekend offered novelty and freedom, although not perhaps for the hapless pedestrians who were the chief casualties of the transport revolution: the year 1934 saw the highest-ever numbers of road casualties – 7,343 deaths and 231,603 injuries. Half those fatalities were pedestrians, although other road-users weren't immune: in 1935 Lord Vernon of Sudbury Hall had a lucky escape when a lorry demolished the car he was driving on the Derby–Uttoxeter road. Eleven years earlier the ten-year-old daughter of Francis and Eleanor Acland was run over and killed at the gates of the Aclands' country house, Killerton in Devon. Leslie Hore-Belisha, Minister of Transport in Ramsay MacDonald's National Government, described the high casualty rates on the road as 'mass murder'.[4]

Undaunted, virtually every country house owner possessed at least one motor car, with stables and coach houses being enthusiastically converted into garages, and advertisements in the 'Situations Vacant' columns of *The Times* for grooms and stablehands giving way to appeals for chauffeur-mechanics, chauffeur-valets, chauffeur-gardener-handymen and even the occasional chauffeuse or chauffeuse-lady's maid ('experienced, careful driver; abstainer').[5] Lord Fairhaven at Anglesey Abbey owned a fleet of Rolls-Royces, one of which was driven into Cambridge every afternoon so that his valet could collect the *Cambridge Evening News*. At Cliveden, Nancy and Waldorf Astor kept five chauffeurs. The Astors' agent, Noel Wiseman, recalled that there was

one for the lady of the house, one for the lord, and they each only drove – I mean Lady Astor's chauffeur wouldn't drive

Lord Astor because Lord Astor had his own chauffeur, and if he wasn't there on the doorstep when he wanted him, if somebody else had taken him you know, there was trouble! They each had their own. Then we had a horse-box driver, who carted the horses about; [and] two driver-mechanics who also included things like mower repairs when they'd got time.[6]

Guests invited to stay at the Duke of Bedford's Woburn Abbey were picked up in London by a chauffeur, who arrived accompanied by one of the duke's footmen. Suitcases were carried in a second of the duke's town cars, driven by another chauffeur accompanied by another footman. ('You never travelled with your suitcase,' recalled the duke's grandson, 'that was not the thing to do.'[7]) On the outskirts of London this little convoy was met by a third and a fourth chauffeur-driven car (from the duke's Woburn fleet), both also equipped with footmen. Guests and luggage were transferred, and then they set off on the final leg of their journey.

There were less orthodox means of getting to the party. Rupert D'Oyly Carte's guests arrived at Coleton Fishacre in Devon by yacht. Lawrence of Arabia, a.k.a. Aircraftman T. E. Shaw, would turn up at Cliveden for the weekend on his 1,000 cc Brough Superior motorcycle. He used to take Nancy Astor for 100-mph rides up and down the drive, leaving Waldorf speechless with rage as Nancy shrieked with joy.

Sometimes guests even arrived by plane. By 1939 thirty-eight municipal aerodromes had been opened in England and Wales, along with around seventy AA-registered 'landing grounds', which ranged from fully equipped airfields, professionally run by flying clubs with hangars and full-time mechanics, to farmers' fields whose facilities extended to a windsock. 'If a circuit of the farm is made,' ran one entry in the AA's *Register of Landing Grounds*, 'the owner, if at home, has consented to move any cattle that may be in the way.'[8] Short-haul passenger services sprang up: by the late 1930s, for example, Provincial Airways offered flights from half a dozen cities to 'the English Riviera': there was a flight time of one hour and fifty-five minutes from Croydon to Torquay, with a car to ferry you from London to Croydon Aerodrome and another to pick you up at Haldon Airfield and take you on to your final destination. 'No tips, no taxi or car fares, no meals to pay for,' declared Provincial's advertisements.

But the 1930s also saw the heyday of the private aviator, and the more intrepid weekender was quite likely to arrive on the lawn in front of his host's country house in his own aeroplane. Convinced that flying would soon become as common as motoring, numbers of hosts and guests obtained pilot's licences, including the Prince of Wales, later Edward VIII, his two younger brothers, the Duke of Gloucester and the Duke of Kent, and Sir Philip Sassoon, who in 1933 in his role as Under-Secretary of State for Air declared that 'The great increase in public and private internal flying . . . is already on its way,' and who proved the point by creating a landing field in the grounds of Trent Park.[9] Charles Winn used to park his biplane on the front lawn of his ancestral seat, Nostell Priory in Yorkshire. Lady Howard de Walden, whose husband leased Chirk Castle near Wrexham from 1910 until 1946, obtained her pilot's licence in 1931, as did three of the couple's daughters. Mother and daughters studied hard at Hendon airfield to obtain their certificates; their plan was to fly back and forth from Chirk to their London house.

Flying was becoming commonplace. In 1933, to spend the weekend with the Londonderrys, Prime Minister Ramsay MacDonald flew from Lossiemouth in Scotland to Aldergrove Aerodrome near Belfast in a De Havilland Dragon then disembarked the Dragon and hopped into a two-seater Moth for the thirty-two-mile final leg down to Mount Stewart. The Londonderrys were also regular flyers: one guest at Mount Stewart remembered that the marquess used to get up early in the morning 'and fly round and round the house at about half past six in his aeroplane'.[10] The marquess and marchioness and their daughter Lady Mairi flew in their private plane from Essex to Mount Stewart one Saturday morning in April 1935 so that they could be present at the annual point-to-point of the County Down Staghounds Hunt Club that afternoon. Unfortunately, Lady Londonderry felt so ill by the time they landed that she retreated to her bedroom while Lady Mairi presented the prizes.

Aviation was still a risky business. In 1935, for example, after his plane was burnt out in a crash at Reading, 23-year-old Arthur Sebag-Montefiore, nephew of the owner of Upton House in Northamptonshire, bought himself a Miles Hawk monoplane, which he crashed while coming in to land at Manston Aerodrome in Kent on his way to his own country house at Ramsgate. This time he wasn't so lucky: he and his passenger were both killed. Just as awful was the weekend party given by Mrs Philip Noble, who in 1931 was waiting with her guests for her husband to fly in for lunch at their Wiltshire country house when a policeman arrived with the news that his plane had crashed in a field in neighbouring Berkshire. Instead of presiding over lunch, Mrs Noble had to leave her guests to eat without her while she went to identify her husband's body.

Having arrived – by train or plane, motorbike or steam yacht or motor car – weekend guests were received with varying degrees of formality. 'We always wanted everybody to enjoy it,' remembered Anne Messel, who grew up close to her grandparents' home at Nymans in Sussex.[11] That desire to put her guests at their ease waned a little in later life. When at New Year 1961 Princess Margaret and her new husband, Anne's son Antony Armstrong-Jones, stayed with her at Birr Castle in Ireland, the other guests included Margaret's ex-fiancé Billy Wallace and her husband's ex-lovers Jeremy and Camilla Fry, which must have been slightly awkward for all concerned. Still, as Robert Boothby said of the atmosphere created by Sassoon at his country house parties, the aim was 'mingled luxury, simplicity and informality, brilliantly contrived'.[12]

Those country house owners who still based themselves in London during the week normally only arrived a few hours before their first guests, the domestic staff going on ahead to prepare in a frenzy of unpacking and organising. Sir Philip Sassoon sometimes didn't arrive at Port Lympne or Trent Park at all; that didn't stop him inviting house-guests in his absence and laying on entertainment for them. At Plas Newydd, the Marquess of Anglesey had only the haziest idea who he had invited to his house parties, so that when he came across people from Sir Michael Duff's neighbouring estate of Vaynol who were using the Plas Newydd swimming pool (with permission) he sometimes mistook them for guests of his own and wandered up to engage them in polite but slightly bewildering conversation.

Guests commonly arrived late on Saturday afternoon (although there were plenty of exceptions to the general rule – visitors usually started to turn up at Cliveden on Friday in time for dinner, while others appeared in dribs and drabs throughout Saturday). On arrival men-servants took up trunks and boxes, while a maid, either the guests' own or one provided by their hostess, would take wraps and items like books and papers which had helped to pass the time during the journey. The arrivals would be offered tea in the hall, and then shown to their room by their hostess, who made sure there were flowers and suitable books beside the bed. Sometimes the guests would be asked for their keys while they were taking tea, so that when they reached their bedroom, they would find cases unlocked and evening clothes laid out ready.

Indeed, deciding what to wear for the house party was always a worry. Laura, Lady Troubridge counselled simplicity: a classically plain tweed coat and skirt, the skirt wide enough to walk in, and the colour a soft tone to melt into the landscape. That was all very well for a walk in the country, but hardly sufficient for a Saturday-to-Monday where everyone dressed for dinner. Lady Marjorie Sterling, whose son Angus would become Director-General of the National Trust, recalled that 'One's clothes were always a worry ... There were very rich people who had marvellous clothes, but on the whole one just scraped through.'[13] The considerate hostess would always make it clear in advance if there was to be any particular activity or event requiring special clothes. It was annoying to be told after one's arrival that there was a plan to go and bathe at some seaside spot when you hadn't brought a costume, or to hear that 'there is a dance on at the so-and-so's and to have no suitable dance frock'.[14]

In the austere 1940s, the process of selecting what to bring (rather than arriving with the entire contents of one's wardrobe) was even more important. 'Today "visiting" often means ... arriving with little packets of butter, sugar, tea and fat and a slight suitcase,' lamented one commentator in 1950, 'instead of the large trunk, the hat-box, the dressing-case filled with lovely clothes which an invitation to stay so often meant.'[15]

Diana Cavendish, who was raised at Holker in Cumbria, and who was never allowed to stay away without a maid, because 'my mother wanted us to be kept an eye on', remembered that her parents' guests would bring lady's maids, valets, even their own sheets. 'Some people considered it an insult, but my mother was delighted,' she said. 'It saved on sheets.'[16] On the other hand Rose Harrison, Nancy Astor's lady's maid, recalled that 'Not everyone would bring his own valet and of course some of the guests didn't even have one, so the footmen would have to look after one gentleman each or sometimes more. It was the same with the housemaids and the ladies, though some preferred to look after themselves.' (Note that 'didn't even have one': when it came to snobbery, the community below stairs frequently had the edge on its above-stairs neighbours.)

Ernest and Wallis Simpson timed their arrival for their first visit to the Prince of Wales's Fort Belvedere in Windsor Great Park – a weekend that would eventually lead to the abdication of Edward VIII and thus change the course of British history – for around six on Saturday, driving down from London in their own car with Wallis's maid in the back. Accustomed to the stuffy formality which they had experienced while weekending at Knole in Kent with Major-General Charles Sackville-West, 4th Baron Sackville, the Simpsons were pleasantly surprised to find the front door of Fort Belvedere opened to them not by a butler or a footman, but by the Prince of Wales himself.

Even more surprising was the sight which sometimes greeted guests arriving to spend a weekend with Maureen, Marchioness of Dufferin and Ava. The Guinness heiress also opened the door herself, but wearing a servant's uniform and treating them to ribald remarks while pretending to be her own maid.

4

MEAT AND DRINK

'I can't think how we all ate so much.'[1] Viscountess Hambleden, who as Lady Patricia Herbert was brought up at Wilton House in the 1920s, spoke for many when she marvelled at the mountains of food which everyone was expected to wade through during a country house weekend. From the moment they arrived until the moment they left, weighed down by a hamper full of sandwiches and biscuits for the journey home, guests waddled from one gargantuan feast to another. At Standen, where a set of scales stood ready to reproach the gluttonous, the young people competed to see how much weight they could put on at a single sitting: the record was five pounds.

It began with tea and cakes in the hall while the cases and trunks were being carried up to one's room. Unless, of course, one was weekending at one of the more 'advanced' country houses, in which case tea might give way to a late-afternoon cocktail, along with plates of canapés – little squares of pastry topped with shrimps or cheese perhaps, or concoctions of sardines, olives and anchovies. 'Small hot sausages, served on tiny sticks, are a popular addition,' noted one mid-twentieth-century commentator.[2]

Then it was time to disappear to one's room and join the queue for the bathroom. Eight or eight-thirty was the usual time for dinner, and evening dress was the norm at house parties until after the Second World War. The practice of men dining in full evening dress – black tailcoat, white waistcoat and white bow tie – had largely gone out of fashion with the First World War, along with powdered wigs for liveried footmen. Serving staff still dressed up, though: in the 1920s the Astors' butler Edwin Lee routinely supervised the serving of dinner at Cliveden wearing a dress livery of navy blue tailcoat, black knee breeches and stockings, and black pumps with gold buckles. The footmen who served the food wore brown jackets and striped waistcoats, and white gloves. Only the butler had bare hands, since he didn't touch the food and served only the wines.

Guests met for drinks in the drawing room a few minutes before dinner. Gilbert Russell and his wife Maud, spending a weekend at Woburn with Gilbert's parsimonious cousin, the 11th Duke of Bedford, were convinced that there would be no cocktails. So they took the precaution of bringing their own thermos filled with ready-mixed martini, which they consumed in the privacy of their bedroom before joining the rest of the party – wisely, as it turned out. Bright Young

Things might indulge in something a little more exotic, although the use of 'uppies' like hashish and cocaine was much rarer than one might imagine from the screaming newspaper headlines. (That said, in the 1940s Chips Channon did surreptitiously add Benzedrine to the cocktails when he gave a dinner party for the queens of Spain and Romania.)

As Christian Scientists, Waldorf and Nancy Astor abstained, not only from 'uppies' but from all alcohol, and they tried without much success to recruit domestic servants who didn't drink.* Lord Astor was particularly hostile towards what he called 'the cocktail habit'. It was the worst form of drinking, he declared in a speech in 1928, because it was concentrated alcohol taken on an empty stomach.[3] Worse, women and young girls were particularly prone to fall victim to its charms. Nevertheless, the Astors always served alcohol with dinner at Cliveden when they had guests; Waldorf relied on his butler to choose suitable wines.

Having reached the drawing room, guests were offered drinks, if they were lucky, and strangers were introduced

* They also instructed their housekeeper and butler, who were in charge of recruiting new staff, not to engage Roman Catholics.

– 49 –

to each other. 'In these days', declared an etiquette manual of 1950, 'it is quite customary for cigarettes to be smoked at this time.'[4] Before going in to dinner the host and hostess discreetly made it clear to each man who was to be his dinner partner. Viscountess Hambleden recalled that it was a tremendous headache for the hostess to give her guests different neighbours at each meal for however many meals there were.

There was no taking the ladies in to dinner when Lady Hambleden was entertaining in her own country house at Henley in the 1930s, she remembered, although this illustrates how social conventions were in a state of flux. At many of the grander houses (and quite a few of the less grand ones) it was still the norm to follow strict precedence, with the host leading in with the woman of highest social rank or perhaps the highest professional status, and the hostess coming in last with the highest-ranking male guest. At the other end of the scale, as Viscountess Hambleden's memories demonstrate, women might go into the dining room first, finding their places by reading the small name-cards lying on their plates, and the men would follow.

The Viscountess again: for 'a really posh dinner party, you would have either thick or clear soup, followed by fish, followed by the *entrée* – chicken or quails. Then you had saddle of lamb or beef; you had pudding; you had a savoury; and then you had fruit.[5] Sherry was served after the soup, hock with the fish, and champagne or red wine with the rest of the meal, until the pudding, when there was claret, sherry, port and Madeira. The interval after dinner when the men stayed on to drink and smoke cigars while the women retired to take coffee in the drawing room – always a source of bewilderment to foreigners – grew shorter and shorter as the twentieth century wore on, although custom and practice varied wildly according to the house and the guest.

Beverley Nichols, who had fond memories of Mrs Greville's house parties at Polesden Lacey in the 1920s and 1930s, recalled that, if Winston Churchill was a guest, the women as they left the dining room knew from bitter experience that

When Winston was at a dinner table with a good cigar in one hand and a better Armagnac in the other, the chances were that they would be left without cavaliers until nearly bedtime, and would have to spend the rest of the evening hissing at each other over acres of Aubusson.[6]

Later, just in case guests felt peckish after their seven-course meal, there would sometimes be supper – perhaps a cold buffet laid out in the dining room with salmon, hams and game pies, and various sweet dishes.

Breakfast was a movable feast. The gong might sound at 8.30 or 9.00 to announce that it was ready – cold meats, game pie and perhaps a dozen hot dishes to choose from. Female guests often had a breakfast tray brought up to their rooms, as did their hostess; the men wandered down as the fancy took them, and it was perfectly possible for breakfast to last until 11.00 or 11.30.

Lunch followed on at 1.00 or 1.30: a soufflé, a main course, cold meats from the sideboard, pudding, cheese and dessert. And after a brief respite, it was time for afternoon tea in the hall. Beverley Nichols conjured up a vivid picture of tea at Polesden Lacey, as everyone rushed about, determined not to incur Mrs Greville's wrath by being late:

Tea is at five o'clock . . . and not five minutes past . . . which means that the Spanish ambassador, who has gone for a walk down the yew avenue hastily retraces his steps, and the Chancellor of the Exchequer . . . hurries down the great staircase, and the various gentlemen rise from their chaises-longues . . . and join the procession to the tea-room. The tea-pots, the cream-jugs, the milk-pots and the sugar basins are of Queen Anne silver; the tea-service is Meissen; and the doyleys, heavily monogrammed, are of Chantilly lace.[7]

The men and women responsible for these daily feasts remained hidden from view for most of the time, although it was considered courteous for regular house-guests to venture down into the kitchen to thank the cook and give her a tip. In the 1930s the Duke and Duchess of Portland used to take their house-guests on a tour of the Welbeck Abbey kitchens after Sunday chapel. They always introduced them to their Swiss chef, Gabriel Tschumi, who had worked at Buckingham Palace for Victoria, Edward VII and George V. 'I often saw the Duke of Gloucester, King Leopold III of the Belgians and his Queen, Princess Alice and the Earl of Athlone,' Tschumi recalled with pride, although he was far too discreet to mention whether or not they tipped him.[8]

The fashionable Victorian habit of recruiting Swiss, French, Belgian or Italian male chefs to run big country house kitchens continued well into the twentieth century. At Cliveden, Monsieur Pappillion was 'the best [chef] in the country and a very nice man to work with', in the opinion of the Astors' butler, Edwin Lee.[9] Pappillion died in 1914, and the chefs who followed him at Cliveden were also French. There was a Monsieur Gilbert and then a Monsieur Lamé, with two or three extra chefs being brought in when there were especially big parties. 'It was more than one's life was worth' to interfere in the kitchen, recalled the Astors' agent.[10] There were five women working in the Cliveden kitchens in the 1920s, a number which was reduced to two in the 1930s, although the wives of estate staff came in to help on special occasions.

Winston Churchill's cook was French by marriage. Georgina Landemare helped occasionally at Chartwell in the 1930s and became the Churchills' full-time cook in 1940, working also at Downing Street and Chequers. She was the widow of Paul Landemare, the distinguished French chef at the Ritz, and seems to have had no formal training, but learned her trade from her husband, who was twenty-five years older than her and a widower with five children when they married in 1909. Georgina was a kitchen maid at the time.

Other households could only run to a cook-housekeeper. At Styles in Sunningdale, Agatha Christie and her husband Archie employed a husband-and-wife couple to cook, clean and serve at table; the gardener's wife came in to help when she was needed. When the Earl and Countess of Coventry entertained at Croome Court, their cook-housekeeper, Winnie Sapsford, was adept at putting aside leftovers for the senior domestics, 'and some', remembered the countess's lady's maid, 'which might not strictly ever have seen the tables upstairs'.[11] This was particularly welcome below stairs, since the meals Mrs Sapsford provided for the servants' hall and the stewards' room weren't particularly appetising. Alfred Latter, the Coventrys' butler, would routinely look down his nose at his dinner, shake his head sadly and ask, 'Winnie, Winnie, what have you done to this?'[12]

5

PLAYING THE FIELD

Foxhunting occupied some country house owners three or four times a week from November to March or April, sometimes more. In old age the 10th Duke of Beaufort, who was Master of the Beaufort Hunt for sixty years, remembered going out six days a week. 'We would get off very early in the morning,' he recalled in the early 1980s. 'Breakfast [was] at six o'clock, because one was out on a horse by half-past six.'[1] The York and Ainsty met regularly at Beningbrough Hall in Yorkshire; the Meynell met at Sudbury in Derbyshire; the East Devon Foxhounds met at Killerton in Devon. Historically, field sports were an integral part of country life, and it was rare indeed for a landowner not to engage in them. Croome Court in Worcestershire was another hunting house: the Earl and Countess of Coventry kept their own pack of hounds there, and the current earl was traditionally the Master, although in the 1930s it was the countess who did most of the hunting, since the 10th Earl's drinking often prevented him from getting up in time to ride.

The Coventrys didn't often entertain, for the same reason; but when they did, their guests were primarily foxhunting men and women. It was common, in any case, for house-guests who enjoyed that sort of thing to be offered the chance to go out with the local hunt. Depending on where a guest was travelling from, and how enthusiastic they were to take the field, they might bring their own hunter, and of course their hunting kit: pink or black coat, white breeches, riding boots and velvet cap or tall silk hat. If they came without a horse of their own, their host might lend them a mount, although the prudent guest would bear in mind the old adage, 'A man may forgive you for breaking his daughter's heart, but never for breaking his hunter's neck.'[2]

Shooting was also part of country house life, and game books listing the members of each shooting party and cataloguing each day's shoot survive at many houses. At Kingston Lacy, Henry Bankes assiduously recorded the names of the guns and the bag not only on his Dorset estate, but also when he shot as a guest on other estates. The big formal shoots tended to take place mid-week, with guests arriving on Monday, shooting on Tuesday, Wednesday and Thursday and leaving on Friday. At Ickworth in Suffolk, the Marquess of Bristol held two big shoots each year, inviting half a dozen male friends, each of whom arrived with a wife, a lady's maid, a chauffeur and a loader, who was often a valet or perhaps a footman. At Ickworth, as at most big country houses, the wives were expected to find some other way of occupying their mornings, joining the men for lunch and then perhaps staying on to watch for the afternoon. There were exceptions. The formidable Duchess of Bedford, who died in 1937 when the plane she was piloting (at the age of seventy-one) disappeared over the North Sea, is still reckoned to be one of the best shots of all time: she once bagged eighty-four pheasants with ninety-four cartridges on her husband's Woburn estate.

Helen Mildmay, who was raised at Flete, a Jacobean house in Devon that had been remodelled by Richard Norman Shaw in 1878, had vivid memories of lunches on the big winter shoots her father held on the estate in the 1920s and 1930s. Luncheon was served by the footmen and the butler, who motored over to one of the keeper's houses; while the food itself, 'lovely stews and that sort of thing', came in hayboxes drawn by the garden horse.[3] There was cider and beer, with cherry brandy afterwards. 'When shooting was over,' she recalled years later, 'we came in and had the most delicious tea, with masses of Devonshire cream, honey, jam, scones and cakes. Everyone would relax and then go to dress for dinner.'[4] At some households it was the practice to place game cards in front of each gun at dinner, notifying them of who had shot what.

It was understood that a shooting guest would receive a present of game to take away – a brace or two of grouse or pheasants, or a couple of brace of partridges and a hare. After a large-scale battue, in which the game was driven towards the waiting guns by maybe forty or fifty estate workers and villagers, the host wouldn't usually miss a pheasant or two from the bag. And a generous host might well give more, as one member of a shooting party recalled in the 1930s:

Coming down from a November fortnight in Scotland, I once embarrassed the railway company (and was venomously surcharged by them) by bringing with me a roe, eight assorted brace of grouse, black-game, capercaillie, and pheasants, and four hefty hares . . . My host, being a good soul, handed the lot to me himself, and did not leave it, like some hotel-keepers with their bills, and some shooting hosts with their tip of game, to the suggestive hands of a head servant.[5]

Even more than the big battue, impromptu rough shooting was high on the list of recreational activities on offer to weekend guests. In this form the shooters walked over stubble or root fields in a line, or even alone, behind pointers or other dogs. There was no need for a small army of beaters, no need for complex preparations. In fact a landowner could wander out on the spur of the moment with a shotgun, a couple of friends and a dog or two and still have a morning's sport. And after the First World War, when taxation, tiredness and a series of agricultural depressions led to the decline of great estates and the sale of let farms to tenants, the popularity of rough shooting increased still further: previously forbidden by law from taking winged game, which technically belonged to the landlord, farmers found that the transition from tenant to owner brought with it a new freedom to shoot on their own land.

Not that rough shooting was confined to farmers. In February 1932 Lord Howard de Walden got up a house party to entertain George V's youngest son, Prince George, who stayed with Howard de Walden at Chirk Castle. The prince was in North Wales to carry out various official engagements, but as soon as they were over he and other members of the house party went shooting, 'the coverts of the Castle estate providing some splendid sport', according to the press, which hopefully pointed out that 'Lord and Lady Howard de Walden's attractive elder daughter was down at Chirk during Prince George's stay.'[6] If there were rumours of a match, they came to nothing – which was perhaps just as well for the Howard de Waldens, considering the prince's predilection for men and cocaine. Five years later he and his new wife Marina were back at Chirk for three days of pheasant shooting with eight other guests.

Chirk often made the society pages. In November 1938 the *Tatler* carried a full page of photographs depicting Lord Howard de Walden, in plus-fours and tweed jacket, with members of another Chirk party: the men with their guns, the women perched on shooting sticks. The caption pointed out a few of the Chirk house-guests, who included Piers and Sarah Legh; Virginia Graham, the daughter of comic poet Harry Graham (author of *Ruthless Rhymes for Heartless Homes*) and a comic writer herself; and the Belgian ambassador, Baron de Cartier de Marchienne, who 'gets shooting invitations by the score'.[7]

Shooting didn't suit everyone. Pauline Trevelyan, whose father Sir Charles Trevelyan loved to shoot on the Wallington estate in Northumberland – 'August 12th was always very much a sacred day,' she recalled – didn't take to the sport at all.[8] Her father's keeper, George Slade, took her out to teach her how to use a gun when she was about twelve. But she cried whenever she hit anything. In the end the kindly Slade had a word with her father and she didn't have to shoot after that. She took up fishing instead.

For those house-guests who looked for alternative forms of recreation there was always tennis. By the 1930s most country houses could boast a tennis court, from vast Baroque mansions like Dyrham Park in Gloucestershire to modest coastal villas like Agatha Christie's Greenway in Devon. There were sunken tennis courts at Cliveden, where George Bernard Shaw photographed Nancy Astor at play; a court in the middle of the lawn at Kingston Lacy in Dorset, where the east front of the house provided a spectacular backdrop; and a Victorian court at Lanhydrock in Cornwall. Lady Denman, the formidable chatelaine of Balcombe Place in Sussex, used to look after the courts herself. Her gardener was allowed to paint the lines, but that was it. The maintenance of the hard surfaces (they were clay courts) and even the weeding was done by her. 'I should think they were as good as any outside Wimbledon,' her daughter recalled.[9]

Country house squash also enjoyed quite a vogue in the 1920s and 1930s, although it was nowhere near as popular as tennis. Lady Howard de Walden built a mock-Tudor squash court at Chirk, and Nancy Astor had a court in the gardens at Rest Harrow, the fourteen-bedroom mansion overlooking Sandwich Bay in Kent where the Astors entertained in the summer; and another on the top floor of their London home, 4 St James's Square. 'Many women are taking to that energetic game, squash racquets,' observed one gossip columnist in 1931, 'mainly, I believe, because it proves to be a wonderful slimming exercise.'[10] Shorts and socks had replaced the skirt on the squash racquets court, the same columnist assured her readers, with a sleeveless jumper and a simple linen belt.

We don't know how many guests availed themselves of the stické indoor tennis court built by Sir Ian Murray Heathcoat-Amory at Knightshayes in Devon in 1907. Once enormously popular, there were purpose-built stické courts in dozens of great houses. Cliveden had one. So did Buckingham Palace. The game made use of the same net, rackets, ball (slightly deflated) and scoring system as lawn tennis, but allowed the players to use the side and back walls of the court. It was invented in the 1870s, around the same time as lawn tennis; but it went out of fashion during the twentieth century to such an extent that there are now only three playable stické courts in the world: one at Corsham in Wiltshire, another in Simla in India, and the third at Knightshayes.

Lord and Lady Bearsted had their own squash court at Upton House in Northamptonshire, and in 1936 Lord Bearsted installed an outdoor swimming pool in the gardens, another feature that figured prominently in house parties all over the country, as a destination on a sunny afternoon, or as the climax of a summer ball, when guests threw off their clothes and swam in the moonlight. Some pools were little more than ponds – the one which the Beale family put in at Standen at the end of the nineteenth century was primarily intended for their young grandchildren, for example. Others were more ambitious. At the turn of the century Lanhydrock in Cornwall boasted two: one, built of granite and quartz rubble, seems to date from the early nineteenth century and was presumably intended as a plunge bath; the other, Edwardian and lined with concrete, was a much grander affair, with a diving board and its own changing rooms.

One of the most famous country house swimming pools was built by Winston Churchill. During Churchill's 'wilderness years' in the 1930s, when he held no government office, he retreated to Chartwell in Kent and dreamed up building projects to pass the time. In 1931, having decided that the two lakes already in the valley were unsafe for swimming, he embarked on the construction of a new pool. Weekend guests were presented with shovels and expected to help with the work: James Lees-Milne, who stayed there around that time, recalled 'Mr C., clad in waders, standing up to his chest in mud and shouting directions like Napoleon before Austerlitz'.[11] The pool wasn't a success: it leaked and, according to Churchill's daughter Sarah, at one point it threatened to slide down the hill. The project was eventually abandoned, but Churchill refused to give up; and in 1933 he tried again, this time wisely bringing in an architect, Charles Goodwin. (Philip Tilden, who remodelled Chartwell for the Churchills in the 1920s, had fallen out with his clients, who accused him of bad workmanship and failing to control the contractors' burgeoning bills.) This new pool was quite substantial, with a maximum depth of over 2.2 metres, and it was heated, 'to supplement our fickle sunshine' said Churchill.[12] In a Rupert-Bear touch, the boiler house chimney was hidden in the trunk of an old oak tree.*

Golf, said Churchill, 'is a game whose aim is to hit a very small ball into an even smaller hole, with weapons singularly ill-designed for the purpose'.[13] Yet golf was perhaps the most fashionable pastime in the years between the wars. It was popularised by the Prince of Wales, whose

* In the 1960s the 16th Earl of Pembroke used to complain that paying visitors to Wilton House would wander into his private garden and then claim they had lost their way, 'even though they're standing there with a cine-camera going full blast documenting me in the swimming pool'.

– 68 –

Conversation piece: an unfinished 1938 painting by Rex Whistler of the family of the 6th Marquess of Anglesey in the music room at Plas Newydd, Anglesey.

Getting from A to B. (*top*) The luggage van at Polesden Lacy, Surrey, in the 1920s. (*centre left*) A bathroom tile designed by Edward Bawden in the bathroom at Coleton Fishacre, Devon. (*centre right*) T. E. Lawrence astride his Brough Superior, 1932. (*bottom*) The Duke and Duchess of York, later King George VI and Queen Elizabeth, on their honeymoon at Polesden Lacey in Surrey, 1923.

(*top left*) A burr walnut veneered cocktail cabinet from the 1930s. Lord Astor condemned cocktail drinking as the worst form of alcohol consumption.

(*above*) The fisherman's tale: Julius Drewe, builder of Castle Drogo in Devon, painted by C. M. Hardie at Faskally in Perthshire.

(*centre left*) Anyone for tennis? By the 1930s, most country houses could boast their own tennis court.

(*below left*) Joyce Heathcoat-Amory of Knightshayes Court in Devon. Lady Heathcoat-Amory was once described as 'the greatest lady golfer of all time'.

(*left*) Croquet on the lawn: a detail from Rex Whistler's 1928 *trompe l'oeil* at Dorneywood in Buckinghamshire, *Ave Silvae Dornii*.

(*below*) The Howard de Walden family while away their time in the saloon at Chirk Castle, in this interwar painting by Sir John Lavery.

(*above*) The games people played: cricket week at Montacute in Somerset, 1905. (*right*) The visitors' book at Chartwell. The book records all visitors from the moment the Churchills moved into their country house until the eve of the Second World War. (*below*) Churchill and friends at Chartwell in about 1928.

(*right*) Clementine Churchill. Her husband built his own swimming pool at Chartwell.

(*top*) An 1898 house party at Knole in Kent. Guests include the Prince of Wales and the Crown Prince of Greece. (*centre left*) Hungry guests taking breakfast after a hunt ball at Kedleston Hall, Derbyshire. (*centre right*) The 5th Marquess of Anglesey (1875–1905) in theatrical costume. Some households were more enthusiastic about amateur dramatics than others.

(*above*) Kaiser Wilhelm II, second from right, posing during a visit to Kingston Lacy in Dorset in 1907.
(*right*) The dining room at Coughton Court, Warwickshire. 'I can't think how we all ate so much,' recalled one house guest.
(*below*) Lord Tredegar and his boxing kangaroo.

The fête champêtre at Osterley Park in west London was one of the great social events of 1939.

(*left*) 'It is hoped that Guests will, if possible, wear 18th Century Dress as a tribute to the Romantic Period in which the House was built.'

(*below*) Host and hostess: the Earl and Countess of Jersey pose in costume beneath a portrait of Francis Child III, one of the earl's ancestors.

passion for the game led to his being made captain of three distinguished clubs, including the Royal and Ancient; and where the prince led, others followed. Advertisements for country houses to let proudly proclaimed that there were links nearby. Even better (from a golfer's point of view, anyway) was the practice of carving up the park to install a nine-hole course of one's own, so that host, hostess and house-guests could step off the terrace and onto the first tee. In 1932, for example, *Country Life* noted that the Mountbattens had let their Sussex seat, Adsdean, while they were abroad. The tenancy agreement included 'the furnished mansion and its exquisite gardens, the private golf course and the shooting over 1,000 acres'.[14] The fact that the golf took precedence over the shooting was indeed a sign of changing times. There was a putting course at Knightshayes Court, a wedding present in 1937 from tenants and estate workers for Sir John Heathcoat-Amory and his wife Joyce, who had been English Ladies golf champion for five consecutive years 1920–4, and British Ladies amateur champion in 1922, 1924, 1925 and 1929. The Astors had a practice course at Cliveden, while in 1926 motor manufacturer William Morris, Lord Nuffield, actually bought the club where he played. He lived in rooms over the clubhouse for seven years, until in 1933 he was able to buy Nuffield Place, a modest country property next door to the links. More than one country house owner refused to invite anyone to a sit-down lunch on Sundays because it would interfere with his round.

The Londonderrys, whose Ulster country house looked out on the waters of Strangford Lough, were keen sailors, and always eager to take their guests yacht-racing, no matter how inexperienced they might be on the water. The 13th Duke of Bedford, then usually known as Ian Russell,* arrived for a visit to Mount Stewart in 1936, still feeling queasy after a rough crossing on the night boat from Stranraer to Belfast, and was dragooned into going out the moment he arrived.

We were doing very well, in fact I think we were winning and suddenly they all shouted at me to let go the something-or-other. So I let go the nearest bit of rope that came to hand and it let down the mast. I had always regarded Lady Londonderry as a very grand respectable gentlewoman, and had seen her at Londonderry House [her London home] at most formal parties. Her flow of language on this occasion was a source of delight to me.[15]

* As the eldest grandson of the 11th Duke (then still living) he also had the courtesy title Lord Howland.

6

GAMES PEOPLE PLAY

When it came to more sedentary recreations, conversation was king. 'In the evening after dinner a discussion starts on the future of England,' Harold Nicolson wrote in his diary during a weekend at Cliveden in 1930.[1] That was a marked improvement on the previous night's after-dinner entertainment, when 'in order to enliven the party, Lady Astor dons a Victorian hat and a pair of false teeth. It does not enliven the party.'[2] For those who were determined to escape such games, billiards was usually available. In more conservative households it was a man's game, but times were changing. The first women's billiards world championship was held in London in 1931. At Standen in West Sussex, designed for the Beale family by Philip Webb in the 1890s, everyone joined in: the youngest Beale daughter, Helen, was an expert player and later taught the game to her young nephews and nieces.

There were always card games. Packs were bought by the gross at the larger country houses, with each pack being used for a couple of nights and then discarded. In the late nineteenth century there was a fashion for baccarat at house parties, the result of the Prince of

Wales's enthusiasm for the game, even though as a game of chance, rather than skill, it had been ruled illegal in 1886 if played for money, even in private homes. A visitor to Sandringham was astonished to see that the royal family played it every night: 'They have a real table, and rakes, and everything like the rooms at Monte Carlo.'³ Auction bridge, another favourite of Edward VII's as prince and king, was also popular, although not in all houses: in 1909 the mistress of Erddig, Louise Yorke, dismissed it as a 'most . . . dissipated game'.⁴ At Cliveden, even though Lord Astor disapproved of gambling, male and female guests frequently stayed up until the early hours playing poker or contract bridge, an American import which, by the 1930s, had supplanted auction bridge as the landed classes' card game of choice. At some houses it was a serious business indeed: the hostess would assign guests to a particular table, and usually played herself. 'It is neither necessary or desirable to make small talk.'⁵ At Cliveden, however, the Astors went to bed, leaving a footman and the groom of the chamber to minister to their guests' wants.

Less challenging to one's morals was the jigsaw puzzle. This had been a nursery staple since the mid-nineteenth century, but between the wars a craze for adult puzzles swept the country. That craze was another US import – by 1933 sales of jigsaws in America were running at *ten million a week* – and it became commonplace for house party guests to be invited to try their hand at a jigsaw laid out on a table in the drawing room or saloon. Film stars were photographed poring over puzzles in their dressing rooms. Advertisements appeared in the *Tatler* for puzzles depicting famous sailing ships; *Country Life* offered jigsaws for hire; Fortnum & Mason sold 2,000-piece puzzles at three guineas. Puzzling was one of the more innocent after-dinner pastimes offered by Edward Prince of Wales at his own country house, Fort Belvedere, while in the 1920s a young gossip columnist called Barbara Cartland scored success with her first novel, which she called *Jig-Saw*.

There is a 1929 painting by Sir John Lavery, depicting Lord and Lady Howard de Walden and their six children relaxing in the saloon at Chirk Castle. Lord Howard de Walden and his son are deep in conversation by the window: in the foreground, two daughters kneel on the floor, engrossed in a game of chess, while a third, the youngest, leans against the back of an armchair. In one corner of the saloon the two remaining daughters play the violin and the cello, while their mother accompanies them on the piano. Apparently Lavery was amused at the way other relations would periodically appear as if by magic and plonk themselves on chairs in the middle of the room, determined to be included in the group portrait: Lady Howard de Walden instructed him to ignore them, insisting that the picture was only to show the immediate family.

The scene finds an echo in an unfinished 1938 painting by Rex Whistler, in which the 6th Marquess of Anglesey, his wife and five of their six children relax in the music room at Plas Newydd. The Marchioness plays the piano while two of her daughters stand behind her, either watching or singing.

Music played a big part in country house life. There is a story of Edward VII meeting a fellow guest on the stairs on the way down to dinner at a house party, and asking, 'What are you going to play tonight?' 'Bridge, I suppose, sir,' said the guest. The King stared and then burst out laughing. 'I took you for the man who conducts the band,' he roared.[6] George V and Queen Mary always dined at Windsor to the accompaniment of a Guards string band who, having struck up 'God Save the King' when the King and Queen and their guests entered the dining room, played throughout the meal, hidden behind a grille in a small chamber next door. Their eldest son preferred the gramophone: after dinner at Fort Belvedere he and his guests would dance round the marble hall to tunes from popular West End musicals. At Mount Stewart the Londonderrys had a pipe band patrolling round the dinner table at night, where – according to the 13th Duke of Bedford, at least – 'the hideous noise stopped all conversation'.[7] Nancy Astor used to regale her house-guests with 'Oh! Susanna' and 'Camptown Races', which she played on a mouth organ. In the early 1930s Lady Acland of Killerton in Devon not only sang in public but also conducted a jazz band at social events in aid of the local women's club.

More organised, perhaps, were the musical per-formances which were a feature of house parties at Wallington in Northumberland. The whole Trevelyan family sang and played instruments, while Lady Trevelyan was a particularly fine pianist. She used to play duets in the drawing room with Sybil Thorndike, a regular visitor to Wallington. The Treveylans' daughter Pauline remembered how her mother 'discovered fairly soon after we went to Wallington [Sir Charles Trevelyan inherited the house in 1928] that one of our parlourmaids, Florrie, had a beautiful voice, so she encouraged her, played for her, sometimes had concerts in the drawing room for her'.[8] The Trevelyans also held big parties at Wallington in the winter. 'We asked people from all over the county,' said Pauline, 'an enormous gathering, for a party with dancing (when it really was dancing) and a certain amount of party games.'[9]

Sometimes the entertainment was laid on by others. House parties were often organised around big local events, like the birthday party at Belvoir Castle which took the Channons to Belton for the weekend in 1935. Lord and Lady Leconfield regularly hosted parties at Petworth during 'Glorious Goodwood', ten miles away; and Cliveden was always full for Ascot week:

Every guest-room would be occupied [recalled Nancy Astor's lady's maid, Rose]. The kitchen and stillroom staff had prepared the cold meats days before for the buffet lunches, for although most of the visitors went racing, some stayed behind to keep her ladyship company. [Unlike her husband, Nancy Astor didn't enjoy horse-racing, and only ever put in a token appearance.] Breakfast was served at eight-thirty and there'd be a dozen hot dishes to choose from. Before this the footmen would have been scurrying along the passages with early morning tea and brass jugs of shaving water. Then downstairs to clean shoes and iron the laces. Some of the ladies' maids, like me, would even wash laces before ironing them.[10]

The social highlight of Ascot was the royal ball at Windsor, which both of the Astors always attended, along with some of their guests. (How did the rest feel about that, one wonders?) Balls, charity events and coming-of-age celebrations were good excuses for house parties. In January 1932 Lord and Lady Bearsted hosted a weekend at Upton, taking their guests to Banbury Town Hall on the Saturday night for the annual ball in aid of Banbury and Horton Hospital. Two years later Frances Drewe, widow of Julius Drewe, brought a dozen guests from Castle Drogo to the Rougemont Hotel in Exeter for the annual Royal Devon and Exeter Hospital Ball, where they were joined by the Lord Lieutenant of the County, the Mayor of Exeter, 'and many other influential people of the city and county'.[11]

Then there were the public and semi-public events that were actually hosted by the owners of country houses in the grounds of their own mansion – fêtes and pageants and political rallies, examples of what the Victorians called noblesse oblige and the twenty-first century would describe as community engagement. They were perfect opportunities to invite friends to stay for the weekend and enjoy the spectacle – or to provide moral support, depending on how enthusiastically the host viewed the appearance on his lawn of several thousand strangers.

Such things were at the mercy of the weather. In July 1936 the monthly meeting of the Drewsteignton Women's Institute was supposed to take the form of a garden party at Castle Drogo, but it was too cold, and the women gathered inside instead, where Mrs and Miss Drewe dispensed tea and they were all treated to a talk on 'Duty towards dumb animals'. It may not have been entirely convincing: the local paper reported that the subsequent 'social half-hour was occupied by an animal hunt in the gardens'.[12]

In the early 1930s Knole was the scene of a succession of ambitious fundraising events, due largely to the efforts of Lord Sackville's second wife, Anne, a New York divorcée with a flair for publicity and a passion for charitable works. One moment she was hosting fifty local businessmen in the Great Hall at Knole, for a fundraising dinner in aid of the local hospital, although 'hosting' is a little misleading: her husband presided over the dinner itself, and only afterwards did she make her entrance and ask for money, 'one wretched female making an appeal to the strong, business-like males', as she told them.[13] A total of £4,722 was pledged on the spot. Weeks later she was presiding with her husband over a Festival of Folk Dance and Song in the gardens, looking on as hundreds of men and women from all over Kent performed dance after dance. 'The dancers never seemed to weary', observed a local reporter, 'while their onlookers sat fascinated by this pleasing revival of dances gleaned from "the good old days".'[14] The success of the festival was reckoned to be a reaction 'from the spirit of jazz'.[15]

The following summer the Sackvilles played host to three big events in the space of six weeks. First came another fundraiser for Sevenoaks Hospital: in the Great Hall before an audience of 200, Cornelia Otis Skinner, an American actress who specialised in dramatic monologues, presented 'for the first time in public' her interpretation of the six wives of Henry VIII.[16] Wearing costumes copied from Holbein paintings, she ran through the lot, from Catherine of Aragon, upbraiding Henry for his neglect, to Catherine Parr, leaving the makeshift stage (erected 'at their own expense' by the boys of Chevening School) with the dramatic cry, 'The King dead! Dead!' Two weeks later Lady Sackville looked on as Princess Arthur of Connaught, being less of a bore than she was at Eaton Hall, one hopes, opened a summer fête in aid of the Waifs and Strays Society. Between four and five thousand people attended the fête: there were dozens of stalls, including 'ye olde cake stall', 'ye bargain shoppe' and 'ye olde joy wheel'; but the highlight of the afternoon was a performance in the Stone Court of scenes from

Shakespeare's *King Henry the Eighth*, with a mixture of professionals and amateurs, 150 performers in all. 'The throne chairs and other furniture were lent from the galleries of Knole.'[17]

That was at the end of June 1931. In July, 15,000 turned up in the park at Knole for the Three-County Conservative Rally, where they heard Stanley Baldwin denounce Ramsay MacDonald's minority Labour government. The house was opened to the public, and entertainments planned for the faithful included 'a motor gymkhana, constituency tugs-of-war and an amusement park containing a variety of novel side-shows'.[18] Baldwin wrote a special message which was attached to coloured balloons to be released by visitors, with a prize going to the balloon which travelled the greatest distance. Responding to a vote of thanks, Lady Sackville told the crowd that she and her husband regarded themselves merely as custodians of something that was meant for all to enjoy. 'That, she was sure, was what the Conservative Party stood for.'[19]

Lord Charles Beresford, who was both a friend of the Prince of Wales in the 1880s and also shared his mistress, recalled how one night at a house party he crept into the bedroom he thought was occupied by his current lover and leapt onto the bed crowing 'Cock-a-doodle-doo!' only to find himself looking down at a surprised Bishop of Chester and his wife. 'The situation seemed very difficult to explain,' and Beresford left the house before breakfast the next morning.[20] More quick-thinking was the male guest who crept into his lover's bedroom one night, thinking her husband was safely playing billiards. He was halfway across the bedroom floor when the husband walked in. 'Hush!' said the man. 'Don't wake her. I thought I smelled smoke, but all is well.' And with that he tiptoed out again, leaving the husband to believe him, or not.

The history of the country house party is filled with stories of guests hopping into bed with each other, or with their hosts or hostesses, or even occasionally with hosts *and* hostesses. It seemed as if everyone was sleeping with everyone else and it was vulgar to mind.

Vulgar or not, divorce was on the increase. In 1918 the number of cases heard at the Probate, Divorce, and Admiralty Division (known colloquially as the Court of Wills, Wives and Wrecks) reached four figures for the first time. Three years later the total number of divorces in England and Wales had risen to 3,522. By 1936, the year in which Edward VIII's determination to marry the divorced Wallis Simpson caused a constitutional crisis, it stood at 5,000. As a result the papers were full of reports of divorce proceedings citing scandalous behaviour at country house parties, where a wealthy elite – whose morals were always viewed with mistrust by the British middle classes – swapped partners with abandon.

'Pyjama Romp' screamed one headline. 'Counsel related the story of a house party ... where the host got all the ladies to dress up in pyjamas and trot round the table.'[21] Another press report in 1920 noted that 'In the spring of 1917 co-respondent had been staying at Sydmonton Court [the Hampshire home of Colonel and Mrs Kingsmill], where he occupied a room adjoining respondent's. One morning a servant found a hair-pin, similar to those Mrs Kingsmill wore, in co-respondent's bed.'[22] The servants also told their master that on another occasion his wife had been seen coming out of the co-respondent's room in her dressing gown. That was enough to establish adultery, and Colonel Kingsmill was granted his divorce.

Even less open to misinterpretation was the case of the publisher Sir Neville Pearson, who was granted a divorce in 1927 after his wife Mary met 'a gentleman of no occupation' named Hordern when the latter was a member of a house party at the Pearsons' country house – and ran off with him.[23]

The practice of bed-hopping was so common – in certain circles, at least – that servants took it for granted that they could encounter guests in the middle of the night, padding along intent on some act of adultery or betrayal. In August 1933 an enterprising burglar dressed himself in pyjamas and made a tour during a weekend house party at Dalmeny House, the Earl of Rosebery's mansion outside Edinburgh. Wandering unchallenged through the bedroom corridors, he managed to steal a pearl necklace worth £4,000, a diamond brooch, a platinum brooch, two watches and two powder-puff boxes.[24] There is a story told of the Bloomsbury art critic Clive Bell (among others) that when he stayed at Ottoline Morrell's Garsington Manor in Oxfordshire there was so much nocturnal activity that he used to make a point of getting up in the night to go to the lavatory several times, just so that he wouldn't seem left out.

7

HOME THOUGHTS

When Monday morning arrived, and the luggage was being piled in the hall while Bradshaws were consulted and cars brought round to ferry departing guests to the station, there were two last tasks for those guests to perform. They must sign the visitors' book, and they must tip the servants. The Astors' formidable butler, Mr Lee, had nothing but contempt for the type of man who rushed around as he was leaving, deliberately avoiding the eye of the butler or the footman who had valeted for him to save himself a few shillings. 'And strangely enough that kind of behaviour generally came from those whom we knew to be loaded.'[1] 'We must give graciously to those hardworking people who assist us in our business and our pleasures', declared Lady Troubridge in *Etiquette and Entertaining*.[2] If you had arrived as a couple (and were leaving as a couple, after all the nocturnal goings-on), it was usual for the husband to tip the butler, and the keeper if there had been a shoot; while the wife left some money on the dressing table – five or ten shillings (25p or 50p) or even a pound note if the servants had put themselves out and one was feeling generous.

Helen Mildmay, who was born in 1907 and raised at Flete in Devon, remembered how 'It was always rather a worrying and embarrassing thing if you were a girl and not married, whether you tipped the butler or not.'[3] So worrying was the whole question, in fact, that in 1933 an author known only as 'Experienced Hands' published an entire book on the subject. *Tips on Tipping* gave advice on how much to give stationmasters, porters and the steward in the restaurant car; taxi drivers, hairdressers, hospital staff, even the members of the band at a private dance. 'If the programme is good, sandwiches and drinks are provided. It is well to remember that brass instrumentalists as a rule have a preference for beer.'[4]

When it came to the country house party, 'Experienced Hands' was full of helpful advice. If there was shooting, ten shillings to the head keeper was perfectly sufficient, whether the bag was large or small, unless one were making a stay of a week or more on a big shoot in Scotland. Then it should be two pounds to the head-keeper, 2s. 6d. [12½p] a day to the ghillie who carried your cartridge bag, and ten shillings a day to your loader. At a three-day shoot at a big country house, 'Experienced Hands' gave the butler ten shillings, and the maid who looked after his grown-up daughter (who also shot) five shillings. There were two chauffeurs, 'but as neither came near us when we stabled and unstabled our own car, they got no tip'.[5] The rates were broadly the same at a smaller country house where father and daughter stayed frequently: the butler got ten shillings and the maid five. On every alternate visit 'Experienced Hands' dropped into the kitchen and tipped the old cook five shillings.

A few houses forbade tipping: at Eaton Hall in Cheshire, the 2nd Duke of Westminster wouldn't allow servants to take anything, but he paid them something himself afterwards, depending on how many people had been staying. So did the Marquess of Londonderry at Mount Stewart. The 11th Duke of Bedford left printed notes all over the place at Woburn telling guests not to tip the servants, although he was notoriously tight with money, and it isn't clear if he compensated his staff for their loss.

Once they were settled back into their first-class carriages, or were being swept towards their Mayfair flats in their gleaming motor cars, how did all those house-guests reflect on their weekends in the country? Did they enjoy being entertained, whether by field sports or fornication or Merrye Englande frolics?

Some found all that fun quite fatiguing. Looking back on the 1920s Judith, Lady Burrell, daughter of Lady Denman, remembered how her mother wouldn't allow weekend guests at Balcombe Place to sit still for a moment. 'If guests arrived on a summer's evening, they probably swam in the pond. On Friday evening they played billiards after dinner, or bridge, and on Saturday they played tennis or golf . . . They always said that they returned to London exhausted on Monday morning.'[6]

That was nothing compared to being harangued by Nancy Astor, who always spent her Saturdays engaged in one kind of sporting activity or another, and who was incensed if she found her house-guests sitting round the fire in the Great Hall or reading in their rooms. 'What do you want to sit around here for?' she would shout. 'Go out! Go out! Look at the lovely day . . . Go out – play tennis – go for a swim in the river. You can always read in London.'[7] (Guests' memories of weekends at Cliveden were at odds with Nancy's own recollections. She convinced herself that 'I never interfered with them . . . My rule was not to appear before lunch.'[8])

Chips Channon enjoyed sneering at his hosts and at his fellow guests. During a visit to Cecil Beaton's Ashcombe in Wiltshire he was introduced, he wrote, to 'an uninteresting couple, the Graham Sutherlands. He is a painter.'[9] During a visit to Cliveden in 1938, 'I really wonder why we came here,' he confided to his diary. 'I hate weekends, and so often feel *desoeuvré* [idle] and bored in other people's houses, and there is nothing so out of date as a 1900 house, which Cliveden is.'[10]

Harold Nicolson found Channon rather vulgar in his relentless pursuit of English nobles and minor foreign royalty. His own flirtation with fascism behind him, he was also appalled by the way the Channons attended the Berlin Olympics and fawned over Ribbentrop and Göring. Unlike Channon, Nicolson's many faults did not include snobbery: writing home to Vita during a weekend with the Astors, he confessed to being overwhelmed by the lavish scale of Cliveden's hospitality. 'Oh my sweet,' he told her, 'how glad I am that we are not so rich. I simply do not want a house like this where nothing is really yours, but belongs to servants and gardeners ... I enjoy seeing [Cliveden]. But to own it, to live here, would be like living on the stage of the Scala theatre in Milan.'[11]

As a young man in the 1930s Ian Russell was taken to Tredegar House by Emerald Cunard, who knew the 2nd Viscount Tredegar. Lord Tredegar, who lived 'surrounded exclusively by Great Danes and handsome men-servants', was a noted occultist: during the Second World War, in which he was unaccountably made an officer in military intelligence, he invited Aleister Crowley to Tredegar House so that the pair could conduct a cursing ritual on Tredegar's commanding officer, after the latter had court-martialled him for giving away military secrets to some girl guides. In less overheated times, weekend guests at Tredegar House ('a fine example of Inigo Jones's work', claimed the press, quite wrongly) might include H. G. Wells, an artist or two, a clutch of well-known society hostesses from Rome and New York, and perhaps Lady Mary Lygon, the inspiration behind Julia Flyte in Evelyn Waugh's *Brideshead Revisited*.[12] Lord Tredegar used to dress up in Tunisian robes to entertain his guests; his constant companion was a foul-mouthed macaw called Blue Boy.

On one particular occasion Tredegar, who also kept a boxing kangaroo, managed to scare the wits out of young Russell by telling fortunes at midnight – while wearing a witch's outfit, brandishing the skeleton of a witch's hand, and encouraging his pet owl to swoop around the four-poster bed in an alarming fashion. The next night, having settled his house party of twenty or so people down to dinner, Tredegar went off to a prior engagement, returning drunk and flying into a rage when he discovered that his guests had closed the windows (this was in the depths of a Welsh winter), thereby shutting out the sound of a choir whom he had invited to sing folk-songs in the garden in his absence.

Russell remembered Tredegar as 'the most extra-ordinary house I have ever stayed at'.[13]

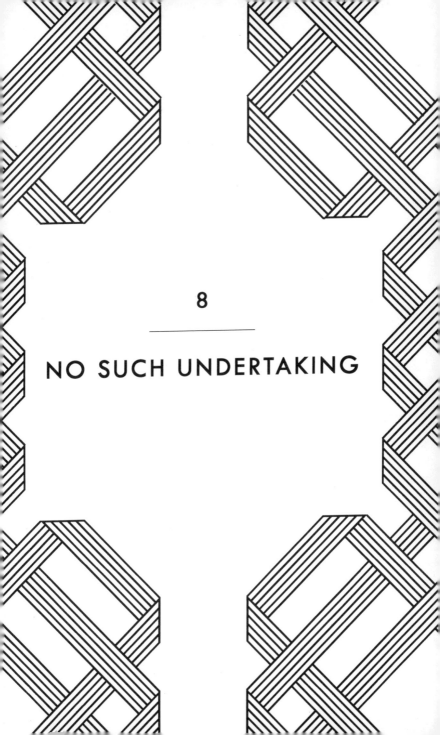

8

NO SUCH UNDERTAKING

Maud Russell loved entertaining. The daughter of a German-Jewish stockbroker who had taken British citizenship in 1885, six years before her birth, she was a wealthy woman in her own right, and her marriage in 1917 to Gilbert Russell, a professional soldier and a grandson of the 6th Duke of Bedford, brought her into one of the most distinguished and long-lineaged aristocratic circles in Britain. ('The idea of marrying a German in wartime tickles me immensely,' Gilbert told his sisters.[1]) Their marriage was a close and loving one, although like so many they lived in a world where love and infidelity existed side by side, strange bedfellows. Throughout the late 1930s and early 1940s Maud kept up a long-running affair with Ian Fleming, seventeen years her junior; and after Gilbert's death in 1942 she began another relationship with the Russian mosaicist Boris Anrep: it lasted until Anrep's death in 1969.

The Russells lived in London in the 1920s, taking short leases on grand country houses like Lord Lothian's Blickling Hall in Norfolk, where they spent their summers and entertained their friends. Then in 1934 they bought

Mottisfont Abbey, a romantically dilapidated Georgian house in Hampshire with a history dating back to the Middle Ages, when it had been an Augustinian priory (never an abbey). Maud Russell brought in Norah Lindsay to advise on the gardens, and commissioned the fashionable architectural firm of Easton & Robertson to bring the house up to modern standards. Maud's 'exquisite revision of the interior' – the words are Christopher Hussey's – included commissioning some astonishing 'Gothic' murals from Rex Whistler, although their working relationship was not a happy one, due in part to her refusal to go along with some of the artist's more fantastic schemes. 'I am just finishing this wretched room,' Whistler wrote in October 1939, describing the project as the most arduous he had ever undertaken.[2]

Throughout the late 1930s the Russells held regular house parties at Mottisfont, travelling down on Friday and going back up to their Cavendish Square house on Monday. They usually moved to Mottisfont for the whole of August, inviting friends and family to stay for varying periods.

And then came the hot summer of 1939. Tension grew over German plans to 'liberate' the free city of Danzig and an increasingly bellicose Japan threatened British interests in the Far East. Italy recalled its ambassador to the Court of St James's. Conscription had been introduced in Britain in May. Churchill gave a speech to the Carlton Club in which he addressed Hitler directly, begging him to 'consider well before you take a plunge into the terrible unknown'.[3] The leader of the British Union of Fascists, Oswald Mosley, asked a rally of his followers, 'Why is it a moral duty to go to war if a German kicks a Jew across the Polish frontier?'[4]

The Air Ministry announced that, having acquired 5,000 acres of land in Wiltshire, it intended to obtain 1,000 more – including part of the Stourhead estate, which was to become a military aerodrome. 'But is this not to be National Trust property?' asked one enraged MP, referring to Sir Henry Hoare's plan to hand over the house and half the estate to the Trust as a remembrance of 'the days that are fled'. He was told by Sir Kingsley Wood, Secretary of State for Air, that in times like these the government had to put the needs of national defence first.[5] A few days later Sir Henry Hoare sent a stiff letter to Sir Kingsley: 'If you compel me to sell you 300 acres of my estate so that you can build a training aerodrome, I shall immediately withdraw my offer to present the mansion house and 2,700 acres of the estate to the nation through the National Trust.'[6] Instead the estate would be broken up and sold.

The Air Ministry backed down.

At Cliveden that summer, Nancy Astor hosted the annual rally of the local branch of the National British Women's Total Abstinence Union. Lord Bearsted hosted a 'Grand Fête' at Upton House in aid of the Edgehill Nursing Association and Hatley Village Hall Lighting Fund: there were fireworks, dancing on the lawn and a comic dog show. At Osterley Park, neither total abstinence nor comic dogs figured as the Earl of Jersey and his film-star wife Virginia Cherrill responded to the prospect of Armageddon by holding one of the year's biggest parties – a Georgian ball and *fête champêtre* in aid of the newly formed Georgian Group. Hundreds of guests arrived in costume on the night of 13 July 1939 to be greeted by footmen in powdered wigs and livery, to hear Handel's Water Music played by an orchestra on a raft moored in the middle of the lake, which was floodlit in purples and greens, and to drink the free beer being distributed from an eighteenth-century beer garden. Most guests came in elaborate fancy dress: Lord Antrim, a Northern Ireland Protestant, chose to wear the bright red robes of a cardinal; Diana Cooper wore a wimple. Maud Russell's eighteenth-century costume was so heavy that she felt faint, and had to lie down on a banquette for a while, 'where, no doubt, the people who saw me said: "There is Mrs Russell, drunk as usual."[7] The Earl of Jersey sported a replica of the costume worn by his ancestor, Francis Child, in a family portrait by Allan Ramsay, while Virginia looked the part in a pale blue lavender and rose net gown designed for her by Oliver Messel. She had a diamond tiara in her powdered grey hair and a diamond bracelet on her wrist, which she managed to lose in the course of the evening.

While Osterley danced the night away, the government was distributing fifteen million leaflets to households all over the country – 'Your Gas Mask: How to Keep and Use It'. Mindful of criticism that the Earl of Jersey and his friends were being incurably frivolous while the world hovered on the brink of war, *Country Life* claimed that the Osterley ball was just what we would all soon be fighting for. 'A great country house ball on a July night is, in a sense, the fine flower of one aspect of civilisation, taking place in surroundings that have perhaps taken centuries to mature and are not seen to such splendid effect but once in a generation.'[8]

When Prime Minister Neville Chamberlain made his broadcast to the nation at 11.15 a.m. on Sunday 3 September, 'We knew where we were,' wrote Maud Russell. After days of listening anxiously to the wireless in her son's bedroom at Mottisfont (the morning-room wireless had gone off for repair), the thought of war filled her with horror. 'I remember the clichés, clap-trap, jokes, soldiers' farewells and misery of the last war,' she confided to her diary. 'But what alternative there is I can't imagine.'[9]

So with the outbreak of war, was the party finally over? It seemed like it. Poor Ralph Dutton had only just put the carpets down and the curtains up in the elegant Regency villa he created out of his father's Victorian pile at Hinton Ampner before he was asked to hand it over to Portsmouth Girls' Grammar School for the duration. He decamped to his flat in Belgravia and a job in the Foreign Office, leaving behind a contingent of strapping young gardeners to maintain the place while they awaited their call-up papers. The headmistress, he later recalled, 'begged that they should be kept away from close proximity to the house as their presence, it seemed, distracted her little charges from their studies'.[10] Dutton wouldn't be in a position to entertain at Hinton Ampner for another six years.*

Other owners kept their country houses while giving up parts of their estate for the war effort. At Dunham

---

* He nearly lost Hinton altogether. In April 1945, after the school had moved out, the Astronomer Royal, Sir Harold Spencer Jones, arrived on the doorstep and announced that he planned to compulsorily purchase Ralph's house as the new Royal Observatory. In the end that honour went to Herstmonceux Castle.

Massey, the park was given over to a US Army camp and then a German prisoner-of-war camp; at Cliveden, Lord Astor offered the use of part of the estate at a rent of a shilling (5p) a year to the Canadian Red Cross (which had been based there in the First World War) and a Canadian Red Cross Memorial Hospital was built in the grounds. The hospital architect was Robert Atkinson, better known for his Art Deco designs for cinemas and for the stunning lobby of the Daily Express Building on Fleet Street. The Astors stored the contents of their St James's Square house in the stables at Cliveden for safety – which was just as well, because the London mansion was damaged by incendiary bombs in October 1940 – and they spent the early 1940s moving between London and Nancy Astor's constituency, Plymouth. Lord Bearsted became a colonel in the Intelligence Corps, helping to organise a British resistance movement in case of invasion; his family moved out of Upton House and their merchant bank, M. Samuel & Co., moved in. Forty evacuees from London moved into Polesden Lacey and Mrs Greville moved out, taking a suite at the Dorchester, where she continued to entertain right up until her death there in September 1942.

None of the hosts and guests who made the country house party such a phenomenon in the 1920s and 1930s was unaffected by the war; but some were less affected than others. The industrialist Lord Aberconway and his wife Christabel continued to entertain at their Welsh country house, Bodnant; Samuel Courtauld was a frequent guest, and mutual friends marvelled in private at the curious resemblance between Courtauld and Christabel's youngest son, Christopher.

Christabel liked to entertain her house-guests by taking them on a tour of the slate quarries at Manod in Snowdonia where the National Gallery had stored its paintings for safety (along with some of Lord Bearsted's most precious works of art from Upton House – being chair of trustees at the National Gallery had its advantages). Christabel and her friends would drive into a high and dripping tunnel, then walk through a door in a brick wall to emerge in huge caves filled with environmentally controlled brick buildings with slate roofs. 'In these huts the pictures were hung or stacked against the wall,' wrote Maud Russell, who stayed at Bodnant with the Aberconways in August 1942. 'A long wooden screen ran down the centre of the huts and on both sides pictures were hung as well. Any picture you want to see can be shown to you at once.'[11]

As well as playing hostess to an assortment of young evacuees, British, Canadian and American soldiers and, in the lead-up to the Normandy landings, a military hospital, Maud kept up her own weekend house parties at Mottisfont throughout the war, entertaining both with Gilbert and, after his death in the spring of 1942, with her lover Boris Anrep. (When in London she also continued to see Ian Fleming, who had obtained war work for her with the Admiralty.) Guests at Mottisfont might include old friends like Eddie Marsh, Sibyl Colefax and Violet Bonham Carter, politicians like Duff Cooper and Churchill's parliamentary private secretary, Tipperary-born Brendan Bracken, and figures from the world of the arts – Cecil Beaton, the ballet dancer and choreographer Frederick Ashton, even the elderly novelist A. E. W. Mason, whose famous 1902 novel of cowardice and courage in wartime, *The Four Feathers*, had a particular resonance in the dark days of the early 1940s. People came and went as they had before the war; if the weather was good they lay about in the gardens, reading and talking. They came together for dinner, and afterwards talked some more or played word games. Maud was fond of persuading a guest to read aloud to the company, although judging from the critical comments in her diary, she rarely chose well. 'I made the mistake of asking Sibyl [Colefax] to read aloud, forgetting one can never hear what she says when she talks,' she wrote on one occasion.[12] On another, Duff Cooper read Tennyson's 'Vision of Sin' 'so badly and so indistinctly that it was grotesque and embarrassing'.[13]

The Mottisfont household was a motley one in the war years. On a single weekend in June 1941, guests included Sibyl Colefax, Frederick Ashton and the American socialite Alice Astor, who after an affair in the late 1930s with Ashton (who was homosexual) was currently married to another gay Englishman. At the same time, five evacuee children, 'a negro refugee from Southampton', and eight officers were living in the house.[14] In the stables there were two more evacuee children, another Southampton refugee and eight batmen, who were presumably there to attend to the needs of the eight officers in the house. The Russells also kept an indoor staff of twelve, all of whom were present for the weekend: Maud's ladies' maid, Adele; Reeve, the butler, who lived with his wife over the stables; three housemaids, a cook and three kitchen-maids, two footmen and an odd-man.

Cecil Beaton was invited over to Mottisfont for one of Maud's weekends at Whitsun 1940. And in many ways the days followed a pre-war pattern. Beaton's fellow guests included Field Marshal Haig's daughter, Doria Scott; Conrad Russell, Gilbert's favourite brother and a close friend of Lady Diana Cooper, although apparently no more than that; Cooper herself; and Frederick Cripps, a lieutenant-commander in the Royal Naval Volunteer Reserve, and his wife Violet, the divorced Duchess of

Westminster. The Cripps fished for trout. Doria Scott knitted. Diana Cooper planned a visit to a bluebell wood with Conrad Russell, and Beaton sketched primroses and painted a watercolour of a picturesquely contorted oak tree. On the surface, it seemed a perfectly normal country house weekend.

But everything wasn't normal. On the Friday, German forces moved into France and the Low Countries. Maud was appalled when Adele brought her the news. She spent Saturday bullying the villagers into accepting more evacuee children. Doria Scott was worried sick because her brigadier husband was a member of the expeditionary force then engaged in a disastrous campaign to liberate Norway from the Germans. Freddie Cripps was on ten days' leave: he would soon have to return to his station on shore at Scapa Flow in the Orkneys, living in a caravan in semi-Arctic cold.

And Diana's husband Duff was absent because, as the party discovered when they gathered round the wireless on Friday evening to listen to the nine o'clock news, Chamberlain had resigned and Churchill was now prime minister. Duff was being considered for a Cabinet post: his appointment as Minister of Information in Churchill's new government was announced in *The Times* on the following Monday.

The perfect late spring weather, the rippling trout streams and the may trees heavy with pink and white blossom were made even more precious, even more vivid, by the contrast between a sunny weekend house party and the knowledge that the Nazis were unleashing fire and destruction across Europe. 'It was a strange feeling staying in this luxuriously appointed house,' wrote Beaton, 'so far and yet so near to all the terrors that had broken loose.'[15]

9

AFTERMATH

In 1945, with the terrors of war finally subdued – only to be replaced by other, darker terrors as the world faced up to the possibility of a nuclear holocaust – the country house parties and balls resumed their leisurely course. It was as if the social upheavals of the mid-century had never happened, as if the war had changed nothing. And perhaps for socialites like Maud Russell and wealthy aesthetes like Ralph Dutton, it hadn't. Inevitably there were changes. In the uncertain early years of the war the Astors had gifted Cliveden to the National Trust, but the family continued to live there until 1965, responding to the post-war shortage of staff by giving the housemaids half a day off a week and every other Sunday, and introducing vacuum cleaners. One of the most spectacular balls of the post-war period was held there in 1957 for Daphne, daughter of Douglas Fairbanks jnr. Fairbanks borrowed Viscount Astor's house for the occasion, and the guest list included the Queen, who danced the night away with Astor and Fairbanks, Prince Philip, Princess Margaret, Princess Alexandra, five dukes and a horde of foreign ambassadors. At midnight Fairbanks put on a firework display below the terrace, inviting tenants, neighbours, and nurses from nearby hospitals to come and watch. 'The Queen on hearing they were there, with her usual thoughtfulness, walked down the steps and stood and waved to them all.'[1]

Also in the 1950s Edith, Lady Londonderry, now a widow, hosted at Mount Stewart one of the biggest post-war hunt balls in Ulster, welcoming 400 guests. And at West Wycombe Park in Buckinghamshire in 1953 Francis Dashwood, elder son of Sir John Dashwood, held 'satanic revels' in the temple on the island in the middle of the lake. Guests were invited to come as inhabitants of the Underworld, or as characters associated with the eighteenth-century Hell-Fire Club, which had held some of its meetings on the same spot. 'Guests entered into the spirit of the party with great gusto,' said a reporter from the *Sketch*. 'There were several beautiful Persephones, numerous Satans and at least two Farouks' (presumably a reference to the sybaritic King Farouk of Egypt, who had just been overthrown).[2] The distinguished economist Professor Roy Harrod came as Mephistopheles, and a youthful John Julius Cooper, son of Duff and Diana, arrived as Orpheus, playing the lyre to his new wife Anne Clifford, a.k.a. Eurydice.

There was no shortage of more sedate country house pleasures. Safely reinstalled at Hinton Ampner, Ralph

Dutton regularly held small parties for his select group of friends. Any weekend might see a gathering of figures at Hinton from the worlds of literature and the arts: Francis Watson, director of the Wallace Collection, perhaps (Dutton was a trustee), and the novelist L. P. Hartley, 'an extraordinarily cosy man to be with', according to a fellow guest; the biographer James Pope-Hennessy, who would stamp off into the garden to sulk if his fellow guests weren't sufficiently amusing; and Ronald Fleming, the society decorator who helped Ralph to create the interiors at Hinton.[3] Ralph was a bachelor, and the redoubtable Christabel Aberconway, who in the years after the war lost both her husband and her lover, sometimes acted as hostess for him. Jane Abdy, wife of the art collector Sir Robert Abdy, brought her cats with her.

Other regulars included Gerry Wellesley, the 7th Duke of Wellington and the architect, with Trenwith Wills, of Ralph's first remodelling of the house; and the art historian Sir Brinsley Ford, who with his wife Joan first stayed at Hinton Ampner in June 1954. Ford later recalled his impressions of the guest bedrooms. He and his wife were put in separate rooms, connected by 'a sumptuously appointed black marble bathroom, with bottles of eau de Cologne and virgin cakes of Floris soap'.[4] Joan was given the Bow Bedroom overlooking the park, a view that Constable might have painted; while her husband had the Yellow Bedroom which faced east, towards the rectangular pool and beyond it 'a Courbet-like group of tall dark trees, all magic and mystery'.[5] Both the Fords had canopied beds which managed to combine character and comfort, hung with pretty old-fashioned chintzes but supplied with 'the most pliable of modern mattresses'.[6]

In the spring of 1955 Frances Partridge and her husband Ralph spent a weekend with Maud Russell at Mottisfont Abbey. Long-time members of the Bloomsbury Group and conventional in their Bloomsburyite rejection of convention – in the late 1920s they had engaged in an uneasy *ménage à quatre* with Ralph's then wife Dora Carrington and his lover Lytton Strachey – they lived in a modest farmhouse at Ham Spray, thirty miles north of Mottisfont. They barely knew Maud Russell, but they were old friends of her lover, Boris Anrep, and it was this connection which had led to the invitation.

The party was quite large, and the Partridges' fellow guests, drawn from the worlds of politics and the arts, included Maurice and Violet Bonham Carter; the art critic

Clive Bell; Ben Nicolson, elder son of Harold Nicolson and Vita Sackville-West; the gentleman architect Paul Hyslop; and the young actress Caroline Blakiston, who would find international stardom thirty years later as the leader of the Rebel Alliance in *Return of the Jedi*.

Frances and Ralph were given a three-room suite with a wonderfully soft bed and the smoothest sheets. And they immediately liked Maud, praising the way she exercised her skills as a hostess. But for Frances, there was something unsettling about the whole weekend. 'I felt a stranger', she wrote in her diary, 'in a world where it is assumed that "we" are innately superior beings to those who minister to us, and deserve to have a better sort of life than they do.'[7]

Frances wasn't alone in believing that this kind of privileged life had no place in modern Britain. By 1949, estate duty was running at a punitive 80 per cent on property valued at more than £1 million. The supply of indoor domestic servants, which had been declining since the First World War, dwindled still further, while rising wages meant that even if one could find the kind of domestic household that had been common at the beginning of the century, one couldn't afford it. That made the post-war country house weekend rather a different experience. 'If the guest is going to do her own room', said one authority on such matters, writing in the late 1940s, 'the hostess might well leave a duster and cloths for her to do it with.'[8] Guests were advised to bring their own soap, their own notepaper and stamps, when they stayed in a country house; they were warned that their hostess might disappear for long periods to work in the kitchen, preparing dinner. Visiting Dudmaston Hall in Shropshire in 1948, James Lees-Milne noted with some astonishment that the Wolryche-Whitmores made do with only two servants: 'Yet these elderly people are cheerful and content.'[9]

Some country house owners, including the cheerful Wolryche-Whitmores, saw the National Trust as a way out of their difficulties. The 11th Duke of Devonshire and the 4th Lord Methuen both tried to persuade the Trust to take their homes, Chatsworth and Corsham Court, but in each case it proved impossible to come to an agreement on the size of the endowment that the Trust required. And even when negotiations were successful, the change of ownership often meant an end to a particular way of life. When the Fairfax-Lucy family gave Charlecote Park in Warwickshire in 1946, they understood the nature of the deal. 'We knew we were parting with four hundred years of family life, and that we'd never again be free to enjoy it in the same way,' said Sir Brian Fairfax-Lucy. 'That was the price we had to pay for retaining our connection with Charlecote.'[10]

For the lucky few, though, the ones with wealth and determination, the party was far from over. Maud Russell, for example, gave Mottisfont Abbey to the National Trust in 1957, but she lived there until 1972, and she continued to entertain as elegantly and enthusiastically as always. John Julius Norwich, who was a frequent guest in the 1950s and 1960s, recalled weekend visits when he was greeted at the door by the butler, and suitcases were whisked away by a footman and unpacked by a maid. In no time at all 'you were sitting in that glorious long drawing-room, frescoed by Rex Whistler, with its blazing log fire and its beautiful Steinway . . . sipping the whiskey sour for which the house was famous'.[11] There was afternoon tea on the lawn, and lazy games of croquet, and after dinner someone would sit down and play that Steinway while the conversation continued around them.

Notes

Chapter 1: Early Arrivals

1 John Nichols (ed.), *The History of the Worthies of England, endeavoured by Thomas Fuller*, 2 vols. (London, 1811), II, 35.

2 Queen Charlotte's diary, 25 August 1789, Royal Collection Trust, https://gpp.rct.uk/GetMultimedia.ashx?db=Catalog&type=default&fname=GEO_ADD_43_1.pdf.

3 Martin Green, *The Delavals: A Family History* (Powdene Publicity, 2009), 42.

4 Mary Elizabeth Lucy, *Mistress of Charlecote: The Memoirs of Mary Elizabeth Lucy 1803–1889* (Orion, 2002), 47.

5 Lucy, *Mistress of Charlecote*, 100.

6 Lucy, *Mistress of Charlecote*, 101.

7 Quoted in Jane Ridley, *Bertie: A Life of Edward VII* (Vintage, 2013), ebook, loc. 2702.

8 *Yorkshire Post and Leeds Intelligencer*, 27 July 1903, 7.

9 Theresa, Marchioness of Londonderry, quoted in Anne de Courcy, *Circe: The Life of Edith, Marchioness of Londonderry* (Sinclair-Stevenson, 1992), 62.

10 *Yorkshire Post and Leeds Intelligencer*, 27 July 1903, 7.

11 *Evening Star*, 28 July 1903, 4.

12 *Observer*, 6 June 1909, 11.

13 Siân Evans, *Mrs Ronnie: The Society Hostess Who Collected Kings* (National Trust, 2013), 48.

14 Ridley, *Bertie*, loc. 9047.

15 *Surrey Mirror*, 11 June 1909, 5.

16 *Aberdeen Press and Journal*, 28 June 1909, 4.

17 *Tatler*, 27 December 1922, 5.

Chapter 2: Who To Ask

1 Maud C. Cooke, *Social Etiquette: or Manners and Customs of Polite Society* (McDermid & Logan, 1896), 83, 107.

2 Lady Troubridge, *Etiquette and Entertaining* (Amalgamated Press, 1939), 11.

3 Merlin Waterson (ed.), *The Country House Remembered* (Routledge & Kegan Paul, 1985), 77.

4 Waterson, *The Country House Remembered*, 82.

5 Anon., *Complete Etiquette for Ladies and Gentlemen* (Ward Lock, 1950), Part 1, 22.

6 Nigel Nicolson (ed.), *Vita and Harold: The Letters of Vita Sackville-West and Harold Nicolson 1910–1962* (Weidenfeld & Nicolson, 1992), 10.

7 Nicolson, *Vita and Harold*, 146. In the same letter she described Virginia sitting opposite, embroidering a design by her sister Vanessa Bell and interrupting Vita's attempts to write by saying from time to time, 'You have written enough, let us now talk about copulation.'

8 Nicolson, *Vita and Harold*, 425.

9 Edward, Duke of Windsor, *A King's Story: The Memoirs of HRH the Duke of Windsor* (Cassell, 1951), 235.

10 Waterson, *The Country House Remembered*, 74.

11 *Londonderry Sentinel*, 19 August 1937, 7.

12 *Illustrated London News*, 18 December 1926, 33.

13 *Tatler*, 31 July 1946, 12.

14 *Tatler*, 24 November 1920, 6.

15 *Falkirk Herald*, 2 September 1931, 5.

16 *Manchester Guardian*, 19 November 1937, 12.

17 Quoted in Norman Rose, *The Cliveden Set: Portrait of an Exclusive Fraternity* (Pimlico, 2001), ebook, loc. 4215.

18 Harold Nicolson, *Diaries and Letters 1930–39* (Collins, 1966), 396.

Chapter 3: Making an Entrance

1 Robert Rhodes James (ed.), *Chips: The Diaries of Sir Henry Channon* (Weidenfeld & Nicolson, 1967), 21.

2 James, *Chips*, 21.

3 James, *Chips*, 21.

4 https://www.dailymail.co.uk/news/article-1247543/How-Thirties-saw-Britain-fall-love-car-nation-road-hogs.html.

5 *The Times*, 16 August 1937, 2.

6 Geoffrey Tyack, 'Service on the Cliveden Estate Between the Wars', *Oral History*, Vol. 5, No. 1 (Spring, 1977), 73.

7 John, Duke of Bedford, *A Silver-Plated Spoon* (Cassell, 1959), 8.

8 Automobile Association Register of Landing Grounds (Automobile Association, 1938), 3.

9 'The Airports Conference', *Flight*, Vol. 25, No. 49 (7 December 1933), 1211.

10 Bedford, *A Silver-Plated Spoon*, 62.

11 Merlin Waterson (ed.), *The Country House Remembered* (Routledge & Kegan Paul, 1985), 69.

12 Robert Boothby, *I Fight to Live* (Victor Gollancz, 1947), 50.

13 Waterson, *The Country House Remembered*, 59.

14 Anon., *Complete Etiquette for Ladies and Gentlemen* (Ward Lock, 1950), Pt 1, 68.

15 Anon., *Complete Etiquette*, Pt 1, 68.

16 Waterson, *The Country House Remembered*, 64.

Chapter 4: Meat and Drink

1 Merlin Waterson (ed.), *The Country House Remembered* (Routledge & Kegan Paul, 1985), 63.

2 Anon., *Complete Etiquette for Ladies and Gentlemen* (Ward Lock, 1950), Pt 1, 26.

3 *Manchester Guardian*, 17 December 1928, 6.

4 Anon., *Complete Etiquette*, Pt 1, 31.

5 Waterson, *The Country House Remembered*, 63.

6 Quoted in Siân Evans, *Mrs Ronnie: The Society Hostess Who Collected Kings* (National Trust, 2013), 118–19.

7 Quoted in Sara Paston-Williams, *The Art of Dining* (National Trust, 1999), 320.

8 Gabriel Tschumi, *Royal Chef: Recollections of Life in Royal Households from Queen Victoria to Queen Mary* (William Kimber, 1956), 160.

9 Quoted in Paston-Williams, *The Art of Dining*, 292.

10 Geoffrey Tyack, 'Service on the Cliveden Estate Between the Wars', *Oral History*, Vol. 5, No. 1 (Spring, 1977), 72.

11 Hilda Newman with Tim Tate, *Diamonds at Dinner: My Life as a Lady's Maid in a 1930s Stately Home* (John Blake, 2013), 148.

12 Newman, *Diamonds at Dinner*, 14–50.

Chapter 5: Playing the Field

1 Merlin Waterson (ed.), *The Country House Remembered* (Routledge & Kegan Paul, 1985), 86.

2 Anon., *Complete Etiquette for Ladies and Gentlemen* (Ward Lock, 1950), Pt 2, 105.

3 Waterson, *The Country House Remembered*, 92.

4 Waterson, *The Country House Remembered*, 92.

5 'Experienced Hands', *Tips on Tipping* (Frederick Warne, 1933), 71–2.

6 *Arbroath Herald and Advertiser*, 12 February 1932, 3.

7 *Tatler*, 30 November 1938, 7.

8 Waterson, *The Country House Remembered*, 98.

9 Waterson, *The Country House Remembered*, 81.

10 *Derby Daily Telegraph*, 3 February 1931, 2.

11 James Lees-Milne, *Midway on the Waves* (Faber & Faber, 1985), 234.

12 Winston Churchill, *The Gathering Storm* (Chiswick Press, 1948), 62.

13 The quote is variously attributed to Churchill, to the American president Woodrow Wilson and to George Nathaniel Curzon, Viceroy of India.

14 *Country Life*, 2 January 1932, xx.

15 John, Duke of Bedford, *A Silver-Plated Spoon* (Cassell, 1959), 62.

Chapter 6: Games People Play

1 Harold Nicolson, *Diaries and Letters 1930–39* (Collins, 1966), 61.

2 Nicolson, *Diaries and Letters*, 60.

3 Jane Ridley, *Bertie: A Life of Edward VII* (Vintage, 2013), ebook, loc. 6847.

4 Clwyd Record Office, D/E.2816, Louisa Yorke's diary, 22 February 1909.

5 Anon., *Complete Etiquette for Ladies and Gentlemen* (Ward Lock, 1950), Pt 2, 65.

6 Jane Ridley, *Bertie: A Life of Edward VII* (Vintage, 2013), ebook, loc. 7410.

7 John, Duke of Bedford, *A Silver-Plated Spoon* (Cassell, 1959), 62.

8 Merlin Waterson (ed.), *The Country House Remembered* (Routledge & Kegan Paul, 1985), 80.

9 Waterson, *The Country House Remembered*, 80.

10 Rosina Harrison, *The Lady's Maid: My Life in Service* (Ebury Press, 2011), 185–6.

11 *Exeter and Plymouth Gazette*, 5 January 1934, 8.

12 *Exeter and Plymouth Gazette*, 24 July 1936, 19.

13 *Sevenoaks Chronicle and Kentish Advertiser*, 30 May 1930, 13.

14 *Sevenoaks Chronicle*, 4 July 1930, 20.

15 *Sevenoaks Chronicle*, 4 July 1930, 20.

16 *Sevenoaks Chronicle*, 19 June 1931, 12.

17 *Sevenoaks Chronicle*, 3 July 1931, 14.

18 *Sevenoaks Chronicle*, 5 June 1931, 13.

19 *Kent and Sussex Courier*, 31 July 1931, 15.

20 Anita Leslie, *Edwardians in Love* (Arrow Books, 1974), 16.

21 *Liverpool Echo*, 21 October 1919, 8.

22 *Pall Mall Gazette*, 29 April 1920, 3.

23 *The Scotsman*, 26 November 1927, 15

24 *Edinburgh Evening News*, 5 October 1933, 10.

Chapter 7: Home Thoughts

1 Rosina Harrison, *The Lady's Maid: My Life in Service* (Ebury Press, 2011), 263.
2 Lady Troubridge, *Etiquette and Entertaining* (Amalgamated Press, 1939), 184.
3 Merlin Waterson (ed.), *The Country House Remembered* (Routledge & Kegan Paul, 1985), 75.
4 'Experienced Hands', *Tips on Tipping* (Frederick Warne, 1933), 122.
5 'Experienced Hands', *Tips on Tipping*, 94.
6 Waterson, *The Country House Remembered*, 81.
7 Norman Rose, *The Cliveden Set: Portrait of an Exclusive Fraternity* (Pimlico, 2001), ebook, loc. 2817.
8 Rose, *The Cliveden Set*, loc. 903.
9 Robert Rhodes James (ed.), *Chips: The Diaries of Sir Henry Channon* (Weidenfeld & Nicolson, 1967), 408.
10 James, *Chips*, 161.
11 Harold Nicolson, *Diaries and Letters 1930–39* (Collins, 1966), 266.
12 *The Sketch*, 21 July 1937, 117.
13 John, Duke of Bedford, *A Silver-Plated Spoon* (Cassell, 1959), 64.

Chapter 8: No Such Undertaking

1 Emily Russell (ed.), *A Constant Heart: The War Diaries of Maud Russell 1938–1945* (Dovecote Press, 2017), 13.
2 Russell, *A Constant Heart*, 21.
3 *The Times*, 29 June 1939, 8.

4 Quoted in Terry Charman, *The Day We Went to War* (Random House, 2010), 38.

5 *Wiltshire Times and Trowbridge Advertiser*, 17 June 1939, 5.

6 *Western Daily Press*, 29 June 1939, 7.

7 Russell, *A Constant Heart*, 62.

8 *Country Life*, 22 July 1939, 56.

9 Russell, *A Constant Heart*, 67.

10 Ralph Dutton, *A Hampshire Manor* (National Trust, 2001), 110.

11 Russell, *A Constant Heart*, 173.

12 Russell, *A Constant Heart*, 131.

13 Russell, *A Constant Heart*, 120.

14 Russell, *A Constant Heart*, 138.

15 Cecil Beaton, *The Years Between: Diaries, 1939–44* (Weidenfeld & Nicolson, 1965), 21.

Chapter 9: Aftermath

1 *Tatler*, 3 July 1957, 6.

2 *The Sketch*, 15 July 1953, 77.

3 Sir Brinsley Ford, 'A Memoir of Ralph Dutton', *Hinton Ampner* (National Trust, 2003), 58.

4 Ford, 'Memoir', 48.

5 Ford, 'Memoir', 48.

6 Ford, 'Memoir', 48.

7 Frances Partridge, *Everything to Lose: Diaries 1945–1960* (Victor Gollancz, 1985), 225.

8 Anon., *Complete Etiquette for Ladies and Gentlemen* (Ward Lock, 1950), Pt 1, 69.

9   James Lees-Milne, *Midway on the Waves* (Faber & Faber, 1985), 120.

10 Robert Harling, *Historic Houses: Conversations in Stately Homes* (Condé Nast Publications, 1969), 56.

11 Emily Russell (ed.), *A Constant Heart: The War Diaries of Maud Russell 1938–1945* (Dovecote Press, 2017), 7.

Acknowledgements

Many people have helped with this book: staff at the wonderful London Library; students and colleagues at the University of Buckingham; curators, custodians and owners of more country houses than I can count; and friends and family in England and Ireland who have offered encouragement and put up with my many foibles. Thanks are due to all of them. And first, last and always, thanks are due to Helen.

Illustrations and Photo Credits

Unfinished painting by Rex Whistler of the Marquess of Anglesey and family. (*Collection of the Marquess of Anglesey*)

The luggage van at Polesden Lacy in the 1920s. (*National Trust/Mrs Greville*)

A bathroom tile by Edward Bawden at Coleton Fishacre in Devon. (*National Trust Images/John Hammond*)

T. E. Lawrence astride his Brough Superior, 1932. (*The Trustees of the Liddell Hart Centre for Military Archives*)

The Duke and Duchess of York at Polesden Lacey in 1923. (*National Trust/Polesden Lacey House Team*)

A cocktail cabinet from the 1930s. (*National Trust Images/ Dennis Gilbert*)

Julius Drewe, by C. M. Hardie. (*National Trust Images/ John Hammond*)

Anyone for tennis? (*National Trust/Anne Chapman & Dave Presswell*)

Joyce Heathcoat-Amory of Knightshayes Court in Devon. (*National Trust Images/John Hammond*)

Detail from Rex Whistler's 1928 *trompe l'oeil* at Dorneywood. (*National Trust Images/John Hammond*)

The Howard de Walden family by Sir John Lavery. (*By kind permission of the Howard de Walden Estate – Photographer/ National Trust Images/Paul Highnam*)

The games peopled played: cricket week at Montacute in Somerset, 1905. (*National Trust Images/Angelo Hornak*)

The visitor's book at Chartwell. (*National Trust Images/ Andreas von Einsiedel*)

Churchill and friends at Chartwell in about 1928. (*National Trust Images*)

An 1898 house party at Knole in Kent. (*National Trust*)

After the ball was over: hungry guests taking breakfast at Kedleston Hall. (*National Trust Images*)

The 5th Marquess of Anglesey (1875–1905) in theatrical costume. (*National Trust/Simon Harris*)

Clementine Churchill. (*National Trust/Amy Law*)

Kaiser Wilhelm II during a visit to Kingston Lacy in 1907. (*National Trust Images*)

The dining room at Coughton Court, Warwickshire. (*National Trust Images/James Dobson*)

Lord Tredegar and his kangaroo. (*National Trust/Reproduced with permission of Newport Museum and Art Gallery*)

'It is hoped that Guests will, if possible, wear 18th Century Dress as a tribute to the Romantic Period in which the House was built.' (*National Trust/Christopher Warleigh-Lack*)

The Earl and Countess of Jersey pose with a portrait of one of the earl's Georgian ancestors. (*Illustrated London News Ltd/ Mary Evans*)

Every effort has been made to trace or contact all copyright holders. The publishers would be pleased to rectify any omissions or errors brought to their notice at the earliest opportunity.